THEN & NOW

BLACKSBURG

OPPOSITE: This view from a hill above Blacksburg around 1880 provides a fitting overview of the contents of this book. Downtown Blacksburg is in the foreground, the church spire marks the Presbyterian Church on Main Street, and the campus of Virginia Agricultural and Mechanical College—Virginia Tech—is in the background. Town and campus meet on Main Street and College Avenue. (DLA.)

THEN & NOW

BLACKSBURG

Terry K. Nicholson
and Terri L. Fisher

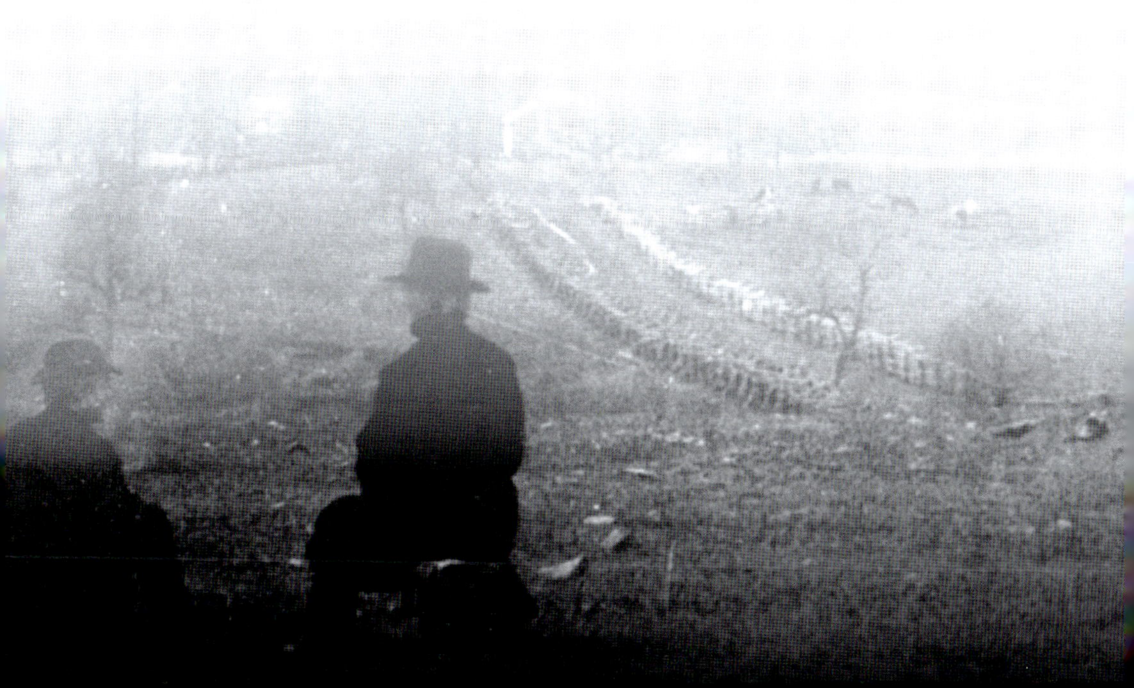

This book is dedicated to our families, who instilled in us a love for the past, encouraged us in the present, and pointed us towards the opportunities of the future.

ISBN 978-0-7385-9241-1

Library of Congress Control Number: 2011943852

Published by Arcadia Publishing
Charleston, South Carolina

Printed in the United States of America

For all general information, please contact Arcadia Publishing:
Telephone 843-853-2070
Fax 843-853-0044
E-mail sales@arcadiapublishing.com
For customer service and orders:
Toll-Free 1-888-313-2665

Visit us on the Internet at www.arcadiapublishing.com

On the Front Cover: The intersection of Main Street and College Avenue is where the town of Blacksburg and Virginia Tech meet. In the early days, the Alumni Gateway marked the transition from town to campus. Today, the intersection is less formal but is still a gathering place for townspeople and students. (DLA.)

On the Back Cover: While other downtowns have seen a decrease in patrons, Blacksburg has remained a vital place because it is a college town. The Lyric Theatre and other businesses on College Avenue cater to students and local residents alike. Diagonal parking has given way to parallel parking, but parking spaces are still usually filled. (DLA.)

Contents

Acknowledgments

We have always had a love for old buildings and what they reveal about the people who constructed them, lived or worked in them, and restored or even demolished them. Blacksburg is a unique example of community preservation. There are 200-year-old buildings and new buildings. There are 45,000 people in town, half of whom change every four years—Virginia Tech students—yet Blacksburg maintains that small-town feel. Our sense of place and community has overcome tragedy and celebrated triumphs. It is truly a special place.

We are grateful to all who helped make this book a reality. Many helped us find historical photographs and identify exactly where they had been taken, which can be challenging when the buildings in the photograph no longer exist. Others suggested where we might find particular photographs.

We want to recognize the staff at Virginia Tech's Digital Library and Archives (DLA), most especially Jane Wills. We are very fortunate in our community to have a facility that is working very hard not only to preserve the photographs and documents of our collective history, but to make them available to the widest possible audience. Many of the historical photographs are from the Virginia Tech collections. Similarly, we would like to thank John Kline (JK), owner of John's Camera and Gentry Studios, a local icon in its own right. John has created his own personal collection of historical photographs from this region and willingly shared. John has created a website with many photographs from his collection: www.johnscam.com.

We would also like to thank the staff and volunteers of both the Blacksburg Museum (TOB) and Historic Smithfield Plantation (SMFD); Rev. Scott West, rector of Christ Episcopal Church (CEC); Jim and Betsy Owen; Joann Sutphin; Belva Collins; Troy Shelor; Craig Little; Nita Little; and the Blacksburg Planning and Building Department and Engineering and GIS Department (TOB).

Finally, we are grateful for the support of the staff at Arcadia Publishing, including Brinkley Gary and Lindsay Carter, who kept us on track throughout the project.

The authors, known locally as "The Terries," took all of the "now" photographs. Where possible, they are taken from the same vantage point as the historical photograph. In some cases, it was more appropriate to take a modern photograph to show a larger context than the historical photograph, so that the reader might recognize other landmarks and thus the location.

Introduction

Blacksburg is the product of waves of activity and people. Each of those waves has left its own mark on the community, beginning with the geological activity forming the mountainous terrain and the numerous springs. Before human habitation, animals followed the streams through the valleys to the plateau where Blacksburg is now nestled. Native Americans followed those animals, hunting and fishing. By the late 1730s, Europeans pushed their way westward into the area and recognized the beauty and the bounty.

Of course, this led to conflict; Native Americans believed the land belonged to everyone, and the Scots-Irish were claiming thousands of acres at a time. One such conflict occurred here in the settlement of Draper's Meadow, centered around the Duck Pond area on what is now the Virginia Tech campus. The Shawnee tribe attacked the settlement, killing five, including James Patton, the key figure in the Scots-Irish push for westward expansion. The tribe also captured Mary Draper Ingles and took her to what is now Kentucky, where she managed to escape and walk home by following the rivers through the mountainous terrain.

The end of the French and Indian War brought a very temporary resolution to these conflicts, establishing the Eastern Continental Divide as the line beyond which Europeans would not settle. Because the Eastern Continental Divide runs right through Blacksburg, the area remained the colonial frontier. But the waves of settlers soon renewed their push, and that boundary was rendered irrelevant. The paths that the animals had created following the rivers and valleys now carried throngs of settlers. Blacksburg became one of the stopping points of the great westward migration.

That second push of Europeans was led by James Patton's nephew William Preston, who quickly picked up where his uncle had left off. In 1774, Preston built an elaborate house and named it Smithfield, after his wife's surname, and moved his large family and his slaves to newly formed Montgomery County. Preston was touting the abundance of opportunity in the area with his own wealth and encouraging others to make the leap.

Preston's strategy worked. As William Black wrote in his 1798 petition to the state legislature for the formation of the Town of Blacksburg, the land was "a piece of ground in a healthy climate, fertile neighborhood, with excellent springs thereon, agreeably and well situated for a small town."

William Black laid out his new town in a very deliberate manner, with five streets running northeast to southwest and five streets running northwest to southeast, creating a grid of Sixteen Squares that still exists today. He donated the 37 acres of land that formed the original town limits. Black envisioned a market town of goods and services for travelers on the migration route. However, his vision was not realized, as most people were only passing through to go farther westward. Frustrated, Black moved farther west himself to start again. William's brother John Black decided to stay in Blacksburg, and his descendants continue to live in the area.

The slow growth changed after the Civil War due to the Morrill Land Grant Act. The act allowed participating states to acquire 30,000 acres of federal land within their boundaries for every member of Congress the state had as of the census of 1860. In Blacksburg, the proceeds from that land's use or sale were to go towards funding an agricultural and mechanical college. A group of forward thinking citizens began campaigning to bring the school to Blacksburg. They offered money, buildings from the struggling Preston and Olin Institute, and other incentives to compete with the University of Virginia, Virginia Military Institute, the College of William and Mary, and other colleges. Their considerable efforts paid off, and in 1872, the first students, all cadets, were enrolled at the Virginia Agricultural and Mechanical College. It should be noted that a separate, segregated school, Hampton Institute, was also funded.

Since its inception, the college has grown exponentially and the town has shared in that growth. There are architectural examples of period styles from each decade, clearly showing the continued expansion. Faculty housing brought an immediate market for new construction, and residences became boardinghouses. Businesses catering to students sprung up downtown, and transportation into the town limits steadily improved.

More growth came as the university transitioned to a coed enrollment in the 1920s, welcomed war veterans in the 1920s and the 1940s, and was racially integrated in the 1960s. More demand for housing and services filled out the town's infrastructure. The abundant "excellent springs" provided the town's water supply up until the 1950s. When several outbreaks of disease were tied to the water supply in the 1930s, after the rapid development of the surrounding landscape, and demand was outpacing available supply, the town of Blacksburg, the university, and the town of Christiansburg partnered to form a water authority with a plan to pump water from the New River to meet ever-expanding needs. "Town-Gown" relationships in a university community can be difficult but often lead to novel solutions to a shared problem.

Since the springs were no longer a resource for drinking water, they came to be perceived as a nuisance and were hastily piped to channel the flow underground. Buildings were constructed directly over the old stream beds. The flaws of this strategy were exposed with flooding and significant impairment of the water quality in Strouble's Creek, so efforts are now geared towards daylighting the streams whenever possible.

The university has also generated other growth within the town, as evidenced by the recent start of Phase II of the Corporate Research Center (CRC). Once again, forward thinking citizens saw an opportunity to reap the benefits of the academic research being done by creating a business incubator. Since 1985, the CRC has constructed 27 buildings and has 18 more planned, and along the way, it has garnered numerous awards and recognition for its leadership amongst university-related research facilities.

Blacksburg thrives on the edge of the frontier, and as new horizons of research and technology emerge, this community leads the way forward.

CHAPTER 1

The Heart of Downtown

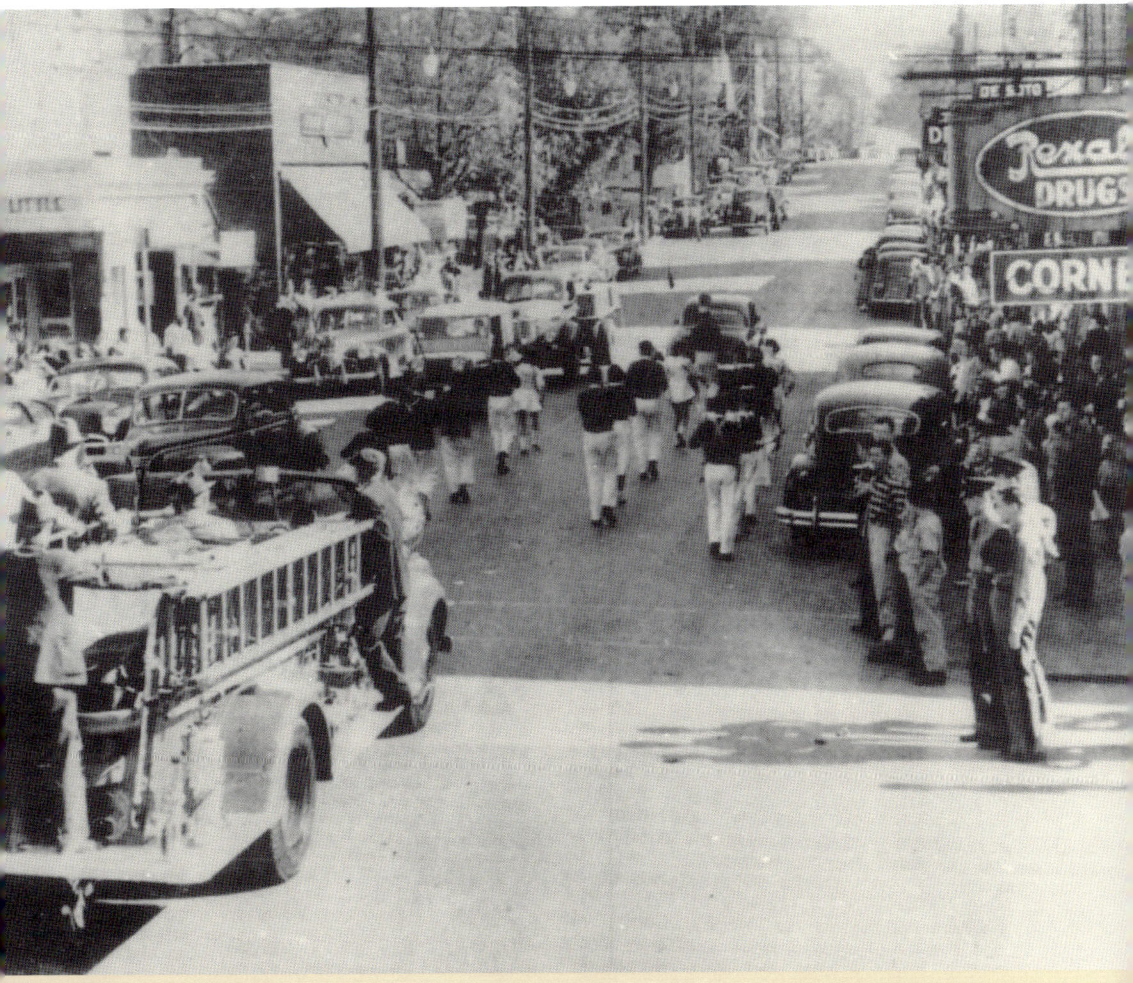

Main Street in Blacksburg is often used for parades, uniting townspeople and college students. This 1940s parade is seen passing through the intersection of Main Street and College Avenue, with the Little Theatre to the left and the Corner Drugstore to the right. Town fire trucks continue to be a major part of every parade. (JK.)

From the Roanoke Street intersection, looking north on Main Street towards campus, this photograph was taken during Virginia Tech's Golden Jubilee, which celebrated the 50 years since the university was formed. To the left is the location of today's Capone's jewelers. The buildings on the right were demolished to make way for the National Bank of Blacksburg and several brick stores. Note the power lines and gravel sidewalks. (DLA.)

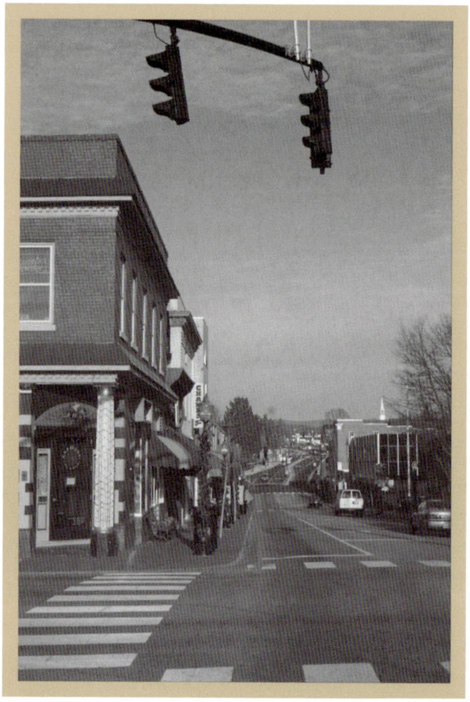

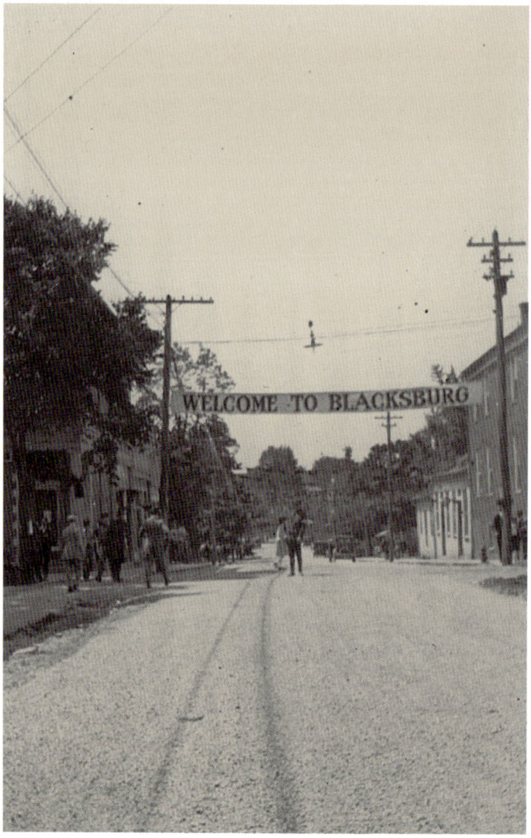

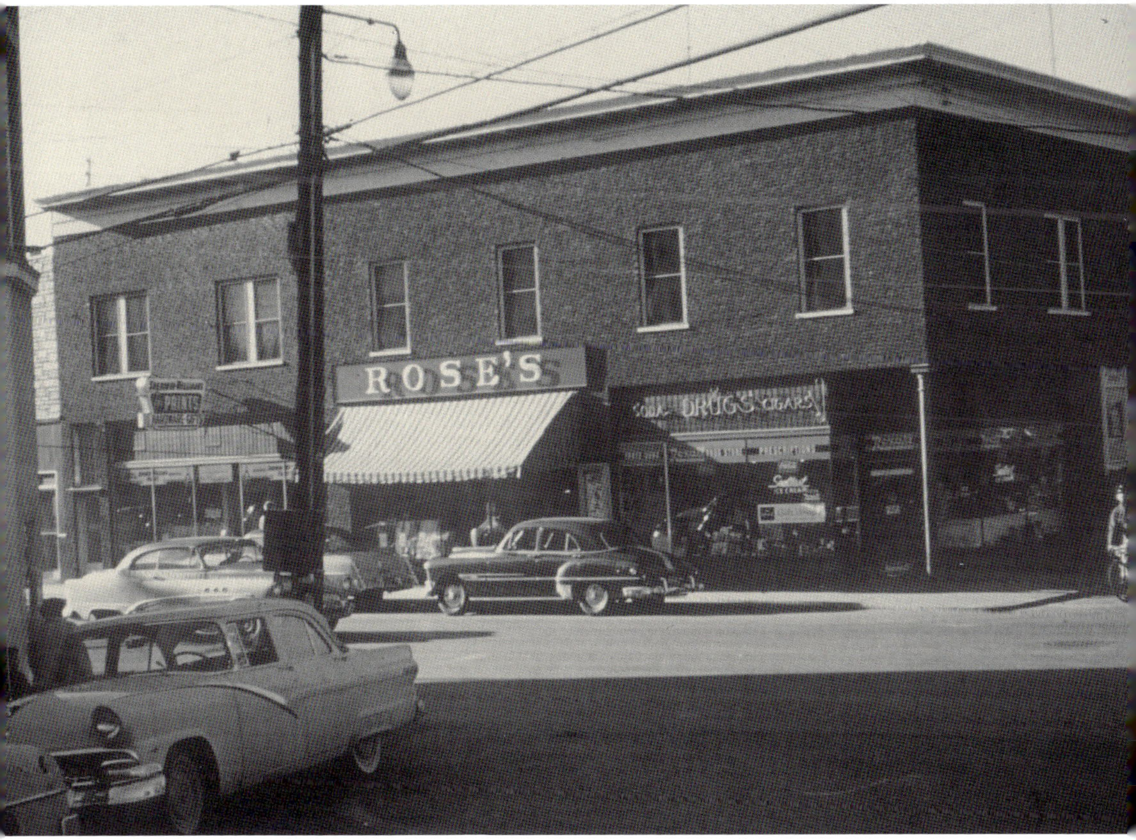

This brick building housing Rose's replaced the wood frame J.H. Woolwine store at the corner of Main Street and College Avenue. In the 1950s, the prominent corner building included a Rexall drugstore selling cigars and ice cream and a hardware store selling Sherwin Williams paint and gifts, making it a one-stop shopping experience. (TOB.)

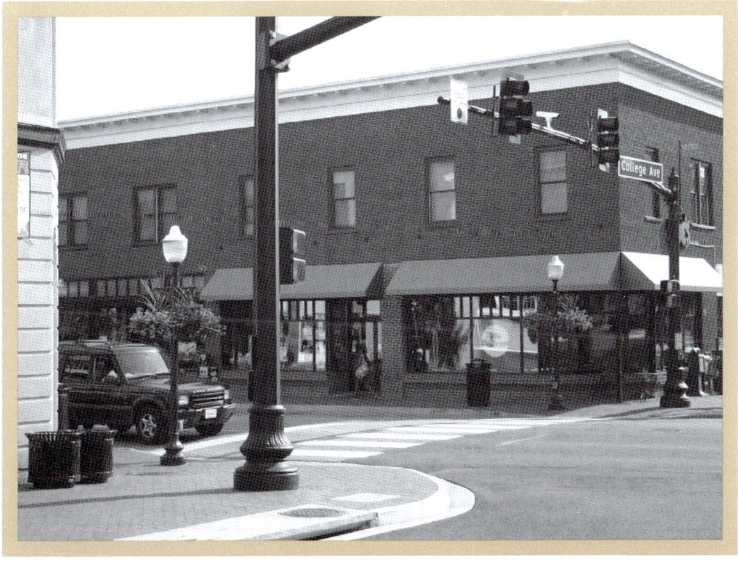

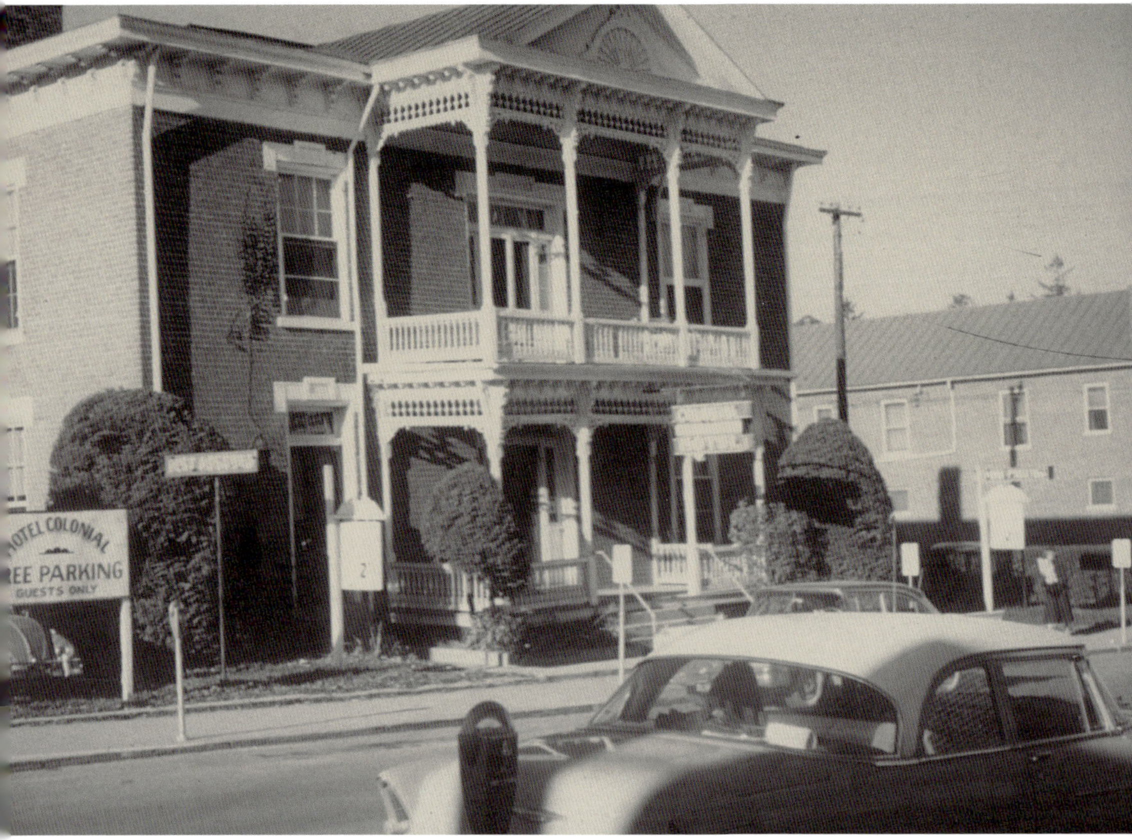

The Hotel Colonial was located on Main and Jackson Streets across from the Blacksburg Post Office. During its life, the building was a residence, a school for girls, a hotel, and home of the Bank of Blacksburg. The Hotel Colonial was demolished in 1961 to build a new Rose's Department Store. The building later became the Grand Piano and Furniture Store and today is known as The Town Centre, home to Mish Mish, Bookholders, and other stores. (TOB.)

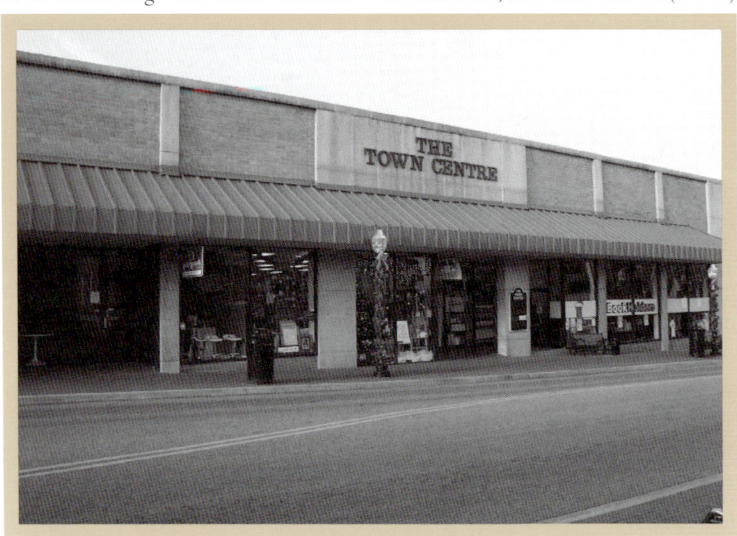

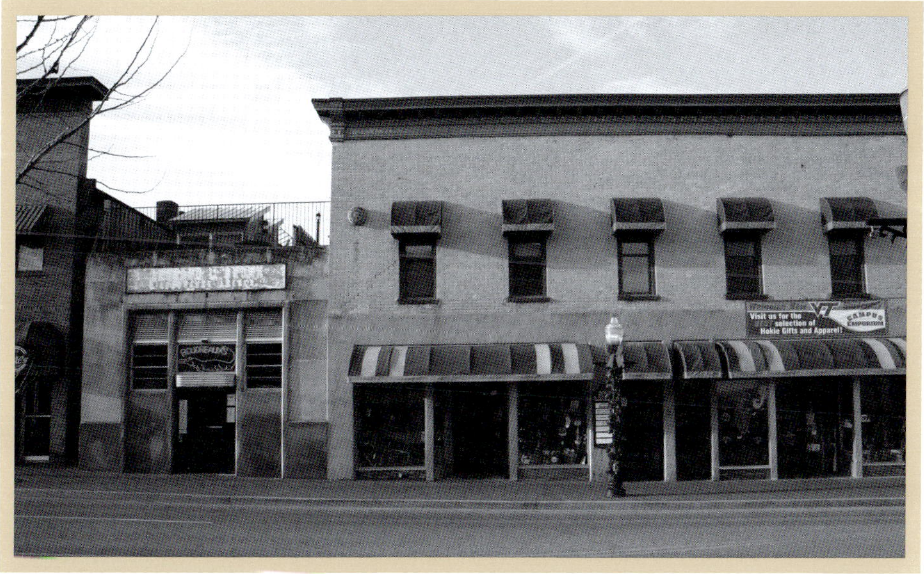

All of the buildings in this photograph still exist but have been slightly modified for their new uses. Just visible on the left is Big Al's Restaurant. The shorter Brown Insurance Agency is now Boudreaux's, and the Western Auto/Tech Drug building is now the Campus Emporium, with offices on the second floor. Such adaptive reuse of older structures in Blacksburg has helped preserve the small town feel of the downtown area. (TOB.)

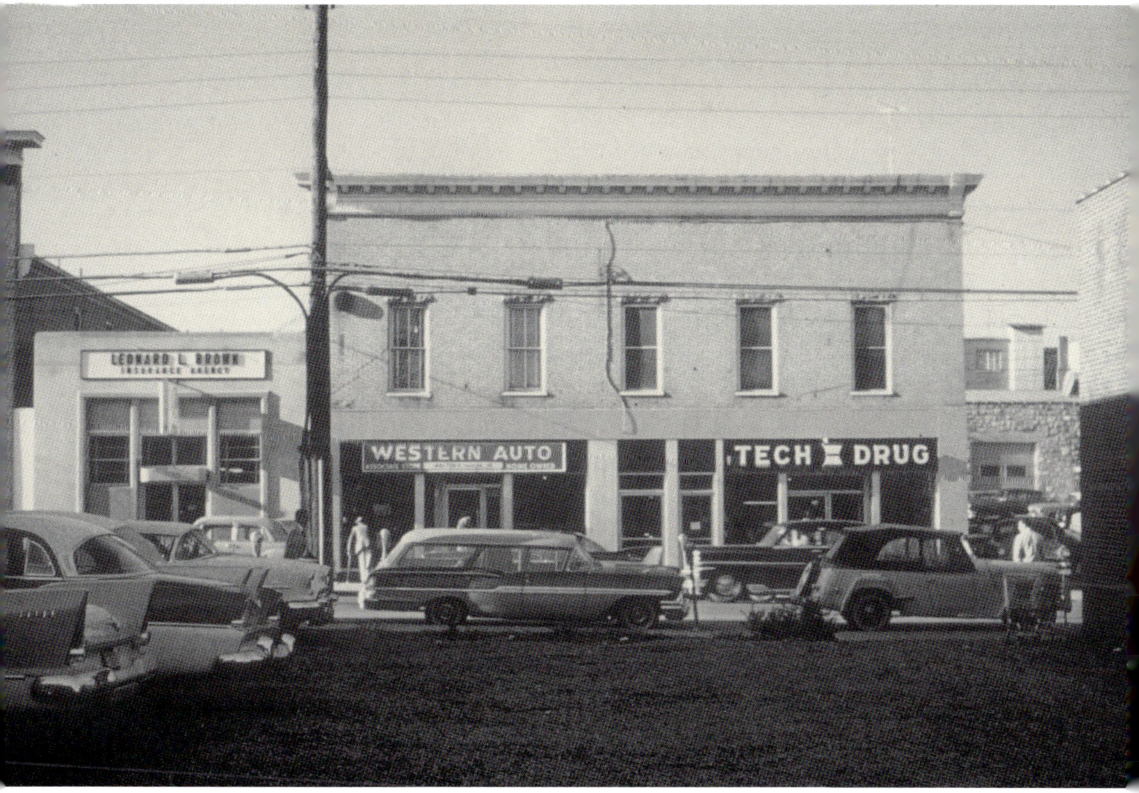

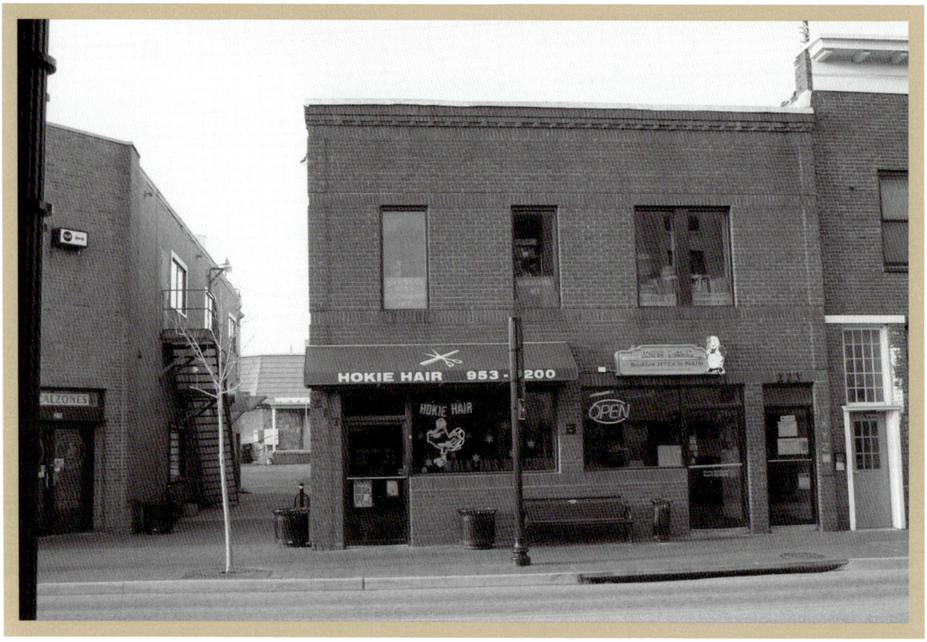

A 1950s view across Main Street shows Star Barber Shop. Notable in the photograph are the telephone booth, a relic of the time before cell phones, and the parking meter, from before Main Street was widened to remove parking. The Veteran Cab Company was in the empty lot to the left. Today, Hokie Hair and Joe's Diner occupy the barbershop building and D.P. Dough is in a new structure constructed on the formerly empty lot. (TOB.)

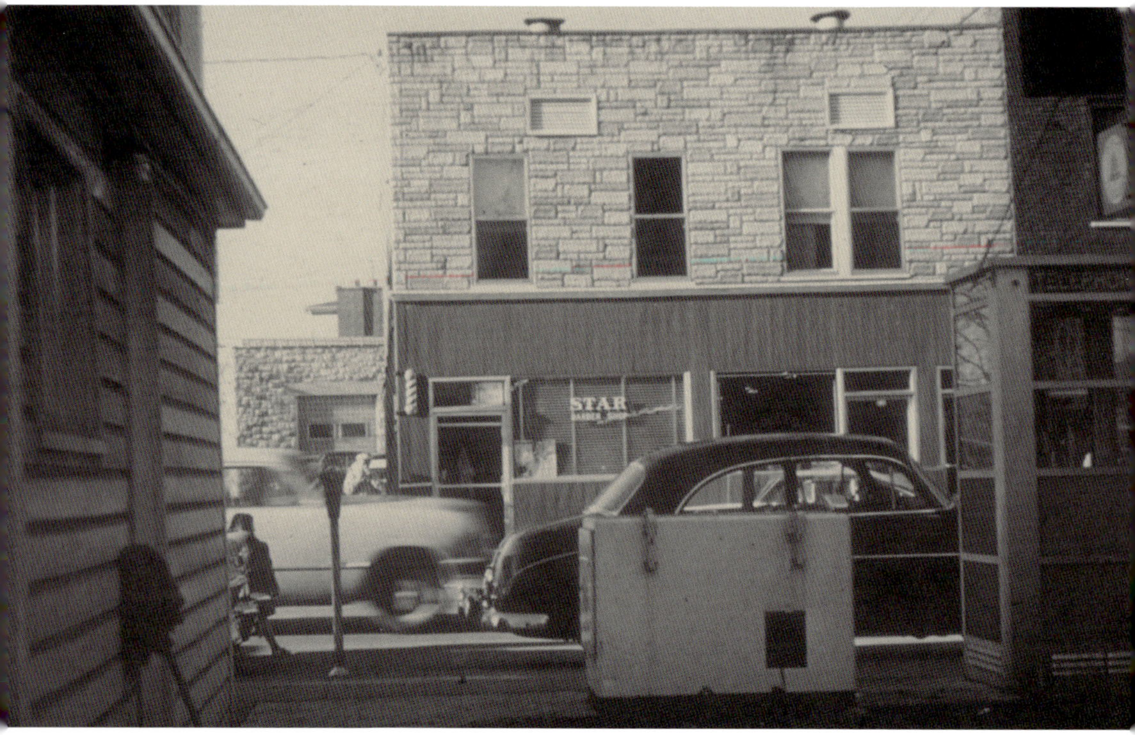

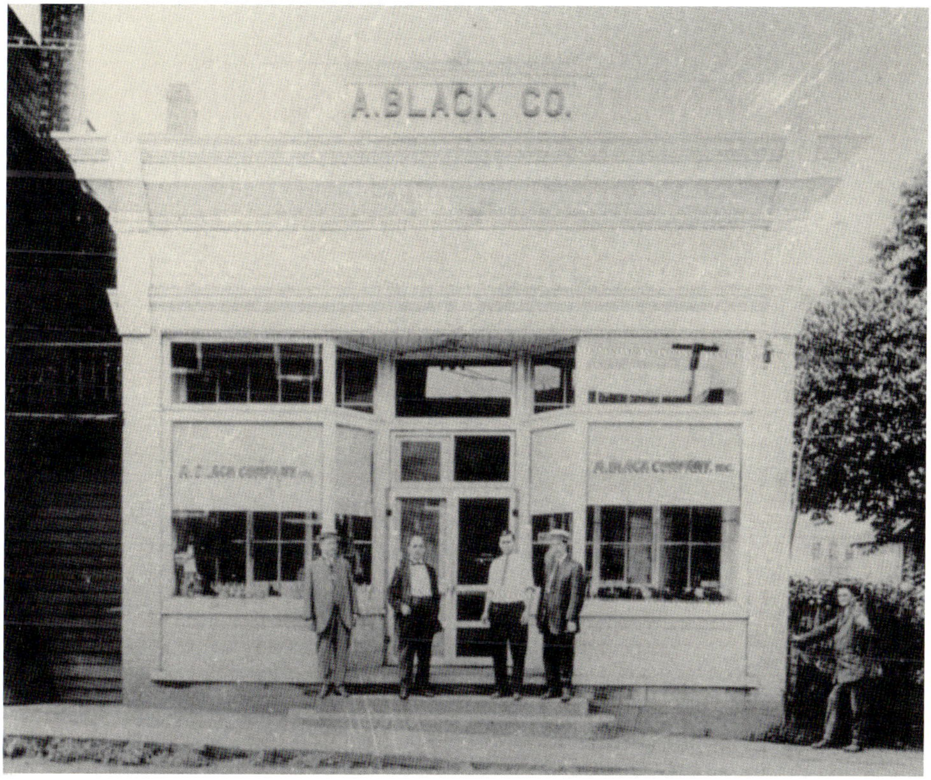

Alexander Black, founding president of the Bank of Blacksburg, ran a general store on Main Street. Retail use continues there today with Mad Dog, which sells clothing and accessories. Black's bank, now NBB, has operated on three different corners of Main and Roanoke Streets in its 120-year history. The first was in the adjacent building, now Capone's Fine Jewelry, and the second was across the street in the currently vacant Art Deco structure. The current downtown branch is the third. (DLA.)

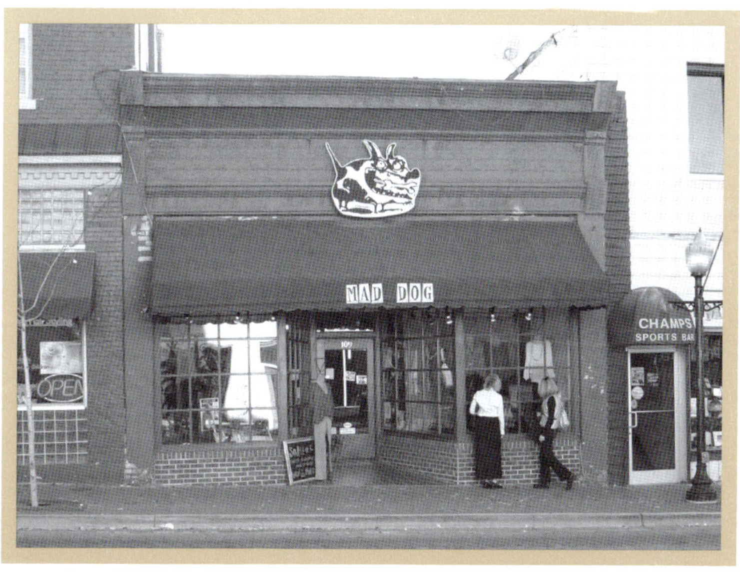

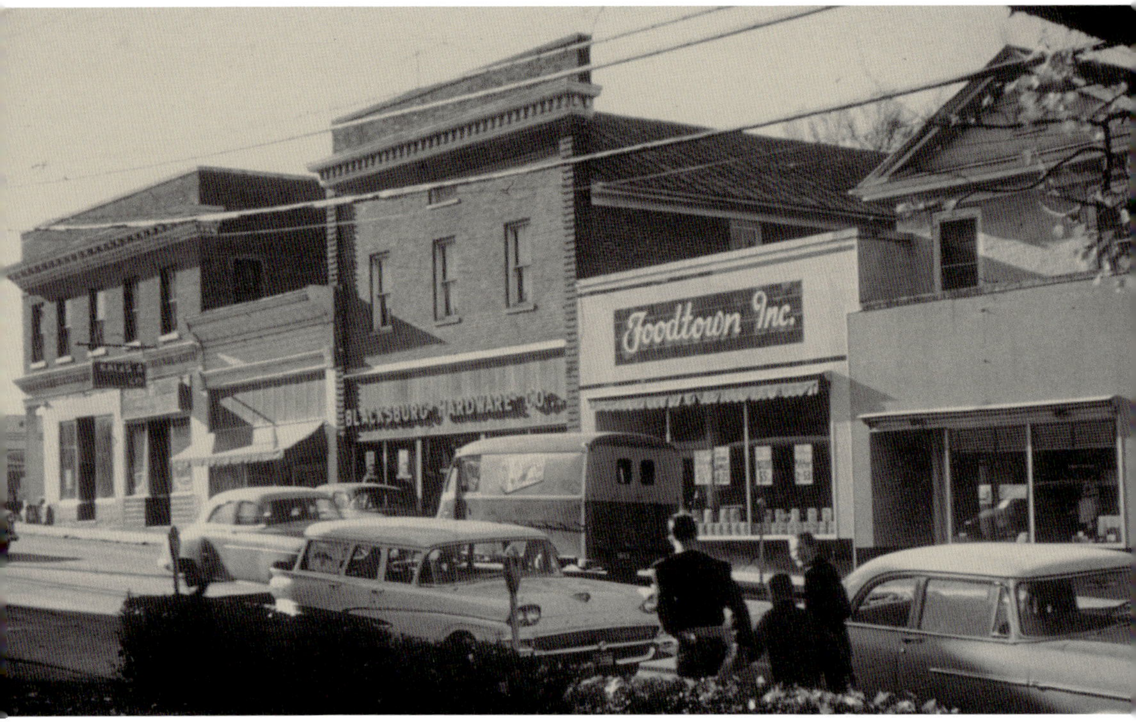

This view, from near the post office on Main Street looking towards the Roanoke Street intersection, shows the similarity of the 1950s streetscape with the current day. The building to the right was lost to fire and replaced by a modern structure around 2000. In the older photograph, the hardware and grocery stores were in this downtown location. Today, residents must go to shopping centers on the outskirts of town to meet those needs. (TOB.)

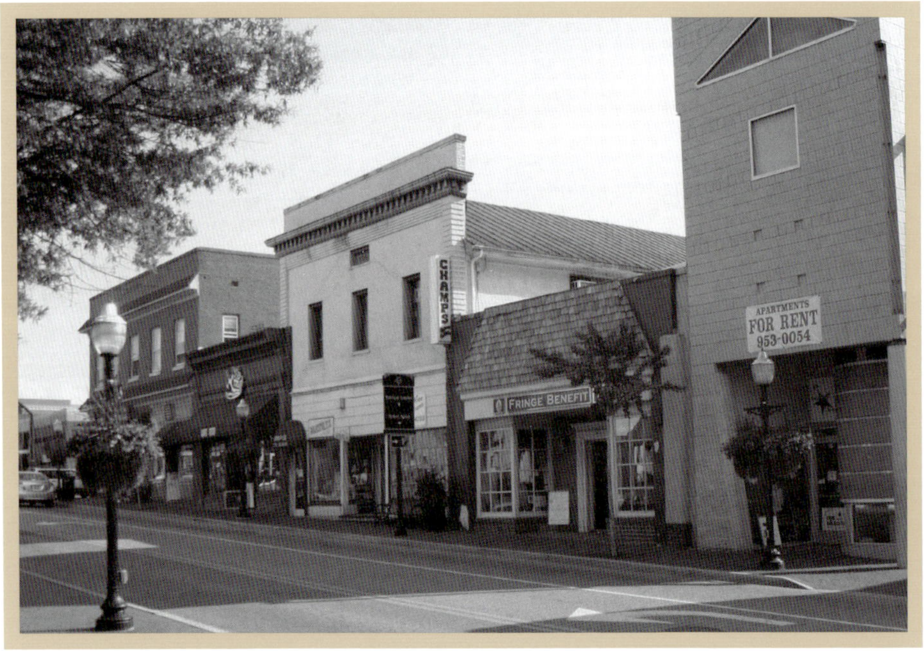

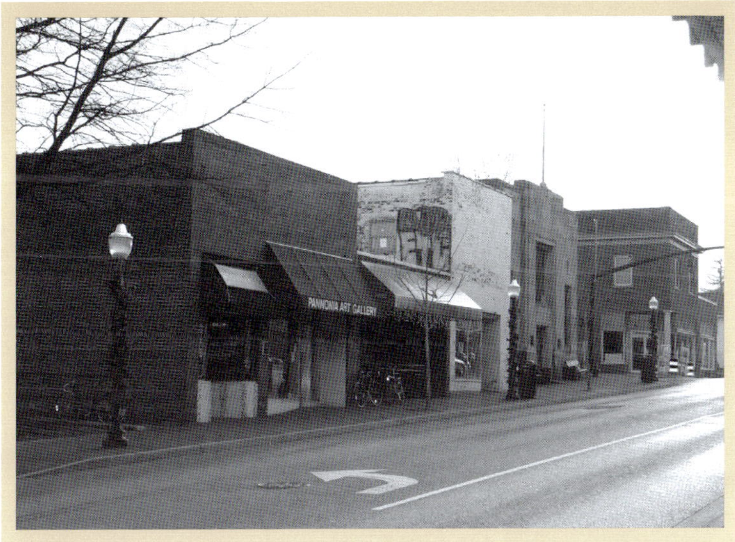

The many cars along Main Street show that Blacksburg was a busy commercial center in the 1950s. Looking south from the post office to Roanoke Street, the block featured The Cottage Restaurant, Tom J. Pierce Real Estate, Louise's Woman's Shop, Blue Grass Market, and the National Bank of Blacksburg. The businesses have changed, but the view is similar today. (TOB.)

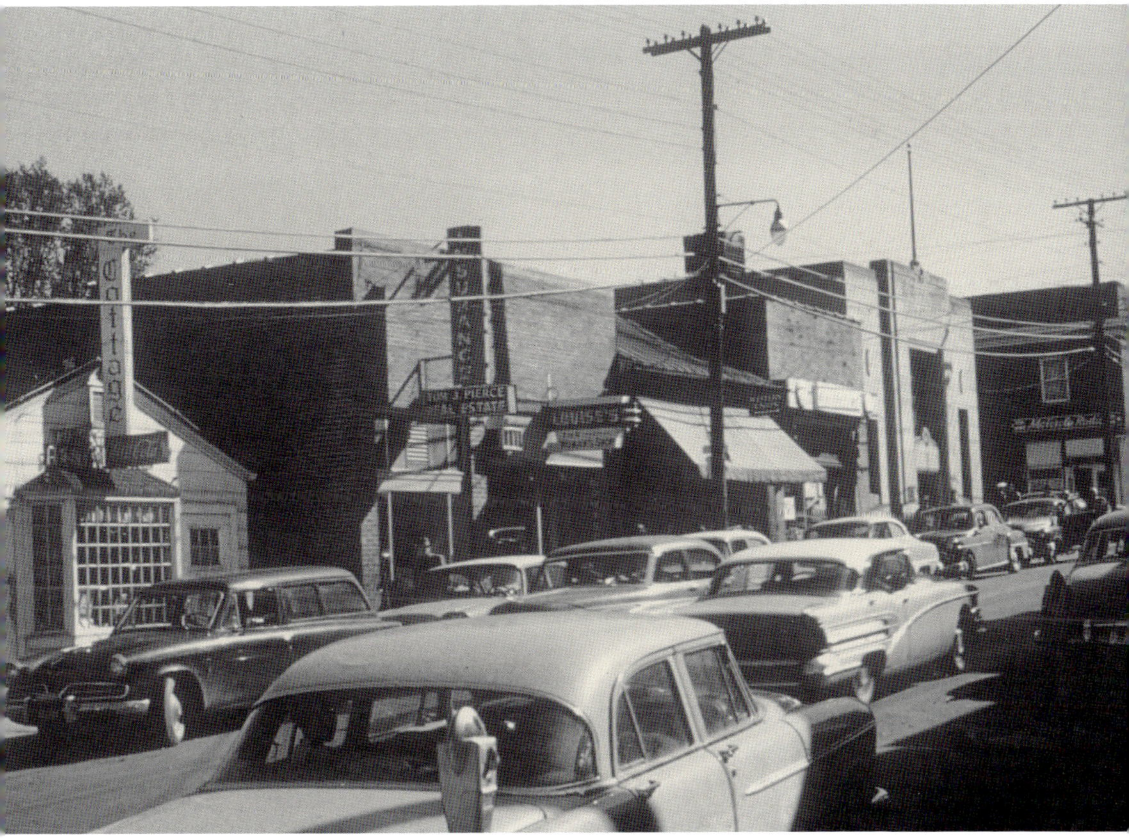

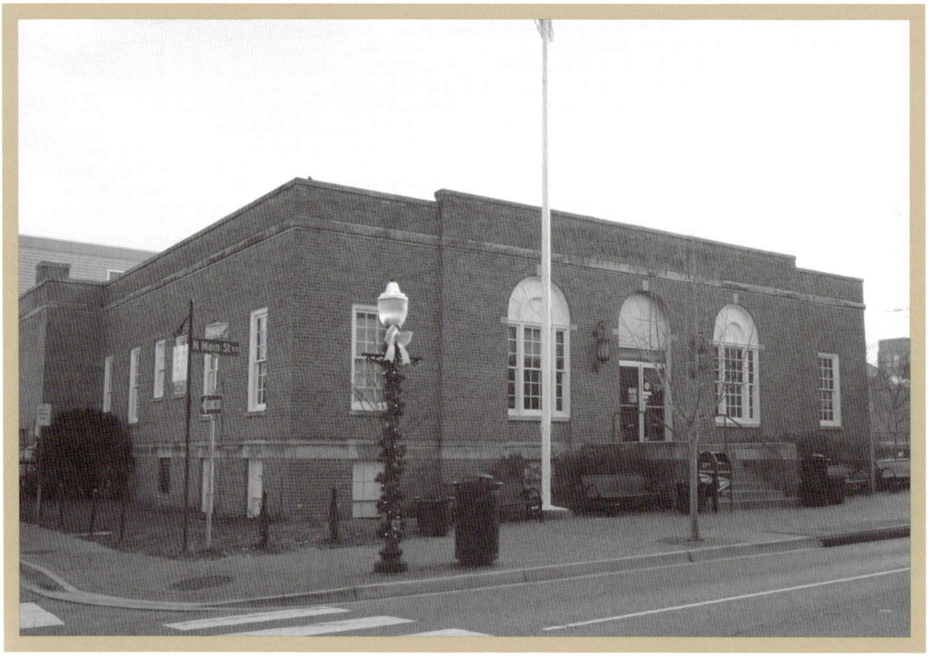

A post office was first established in "Blacksburgh" in 1827. The name was changed to Blacksburg in 1893. The post office was located in many different places on Main Street and College Avenue before the present building was constructed on Main Street in 1935. Though the main Blacksburg Post Office is now located on University City Boulevard, the Main Street branch remains busy with the pedestrian traffic of students and downtown businesses. (DLA.)

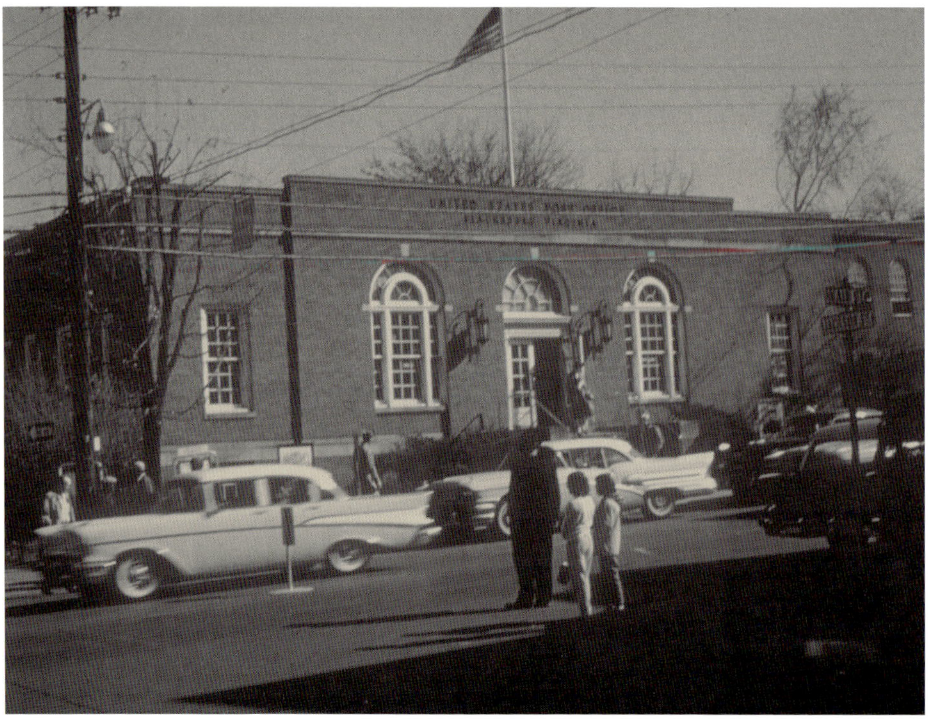

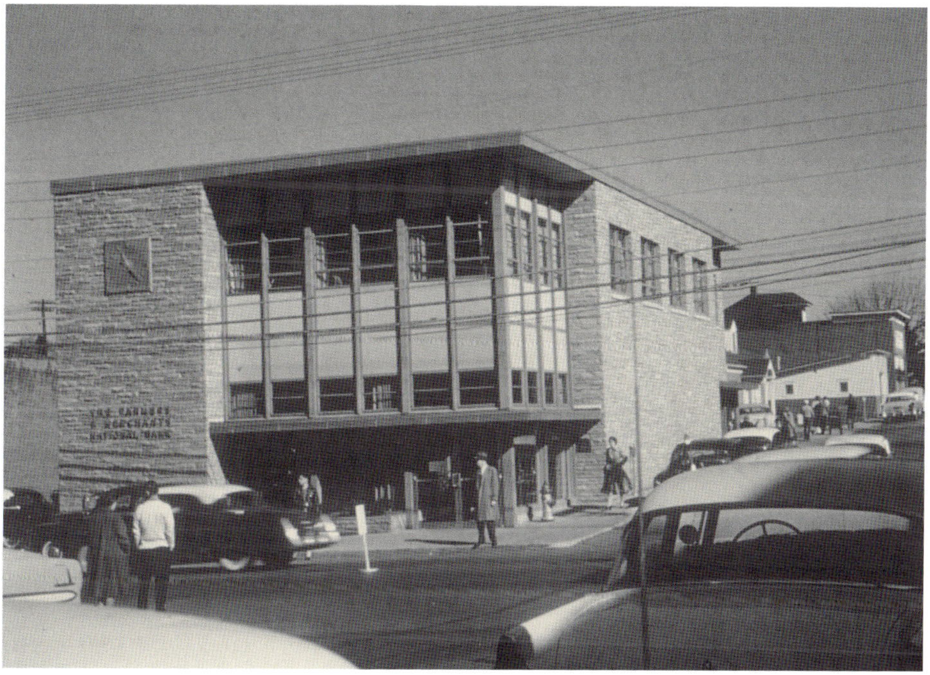

The Farmers and Merchants National Bank sat at the corner of Main and Jackson Streets in the 1950s. The building has undergone facade changes and many name changes as banks have merged throughout the years, but it has remained a bank throughout. Today, it is a Wells Fargo branch. Though the trees hide the other buildings on Jackson Street, they remain the same as in the earlier photograph. (TOB.)

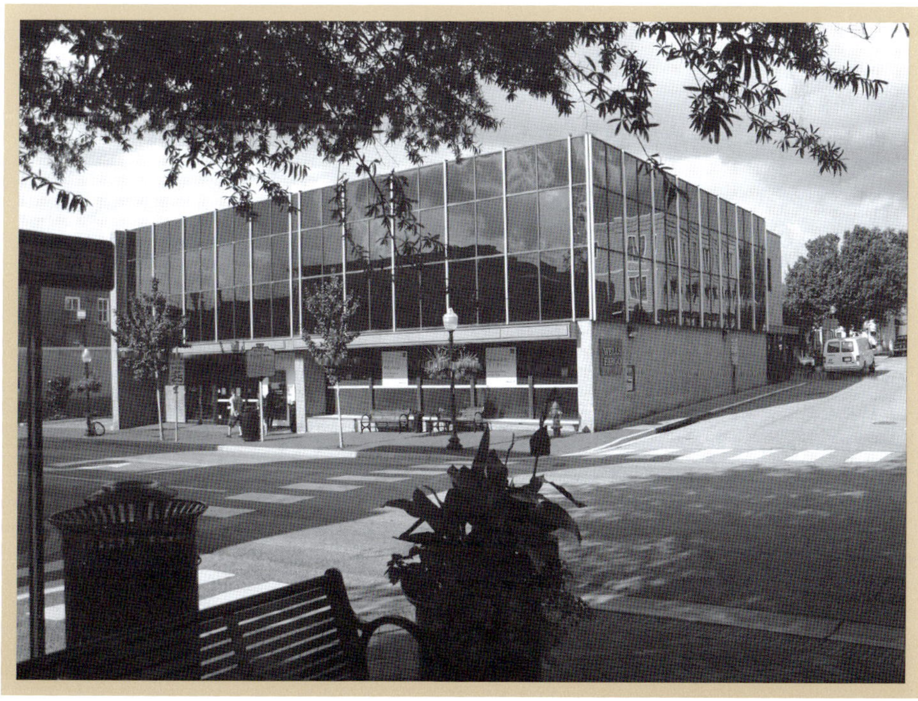

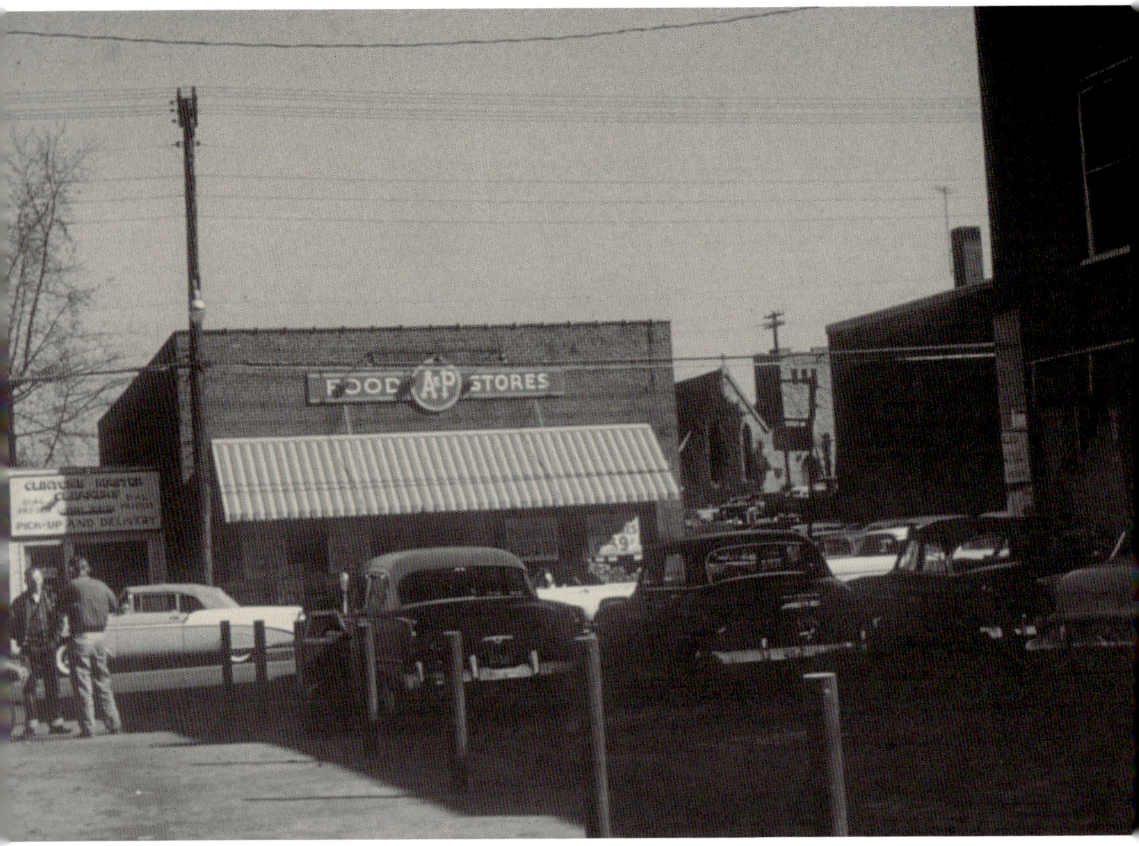

Until the 1960s, grocery stores, like the A&P on Main Street, were much smaller than they are today and often located downtown. Christ Episcopal Church can also be seen in the background. (TOB.)

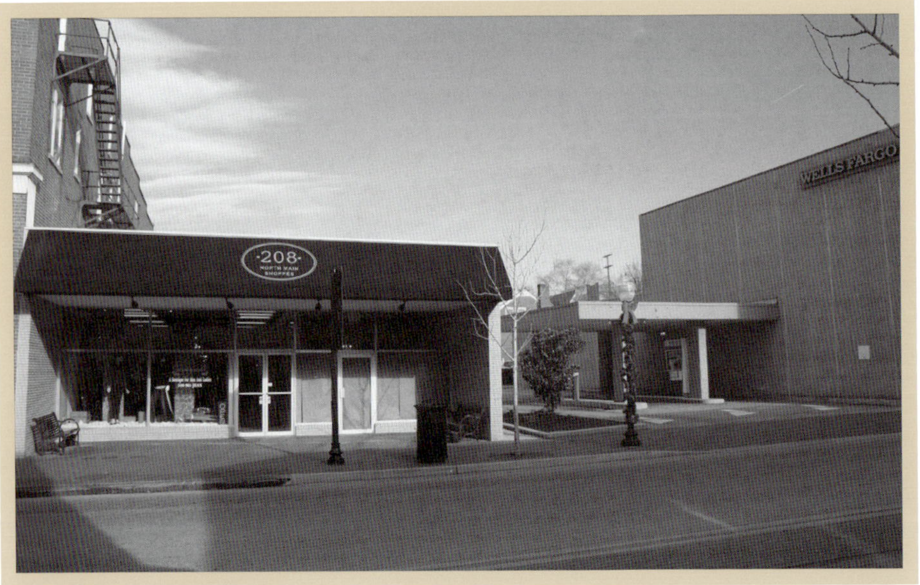

CHAPTER 2

MUNICIPAL-OWNED HISTORIC BUILDINGS

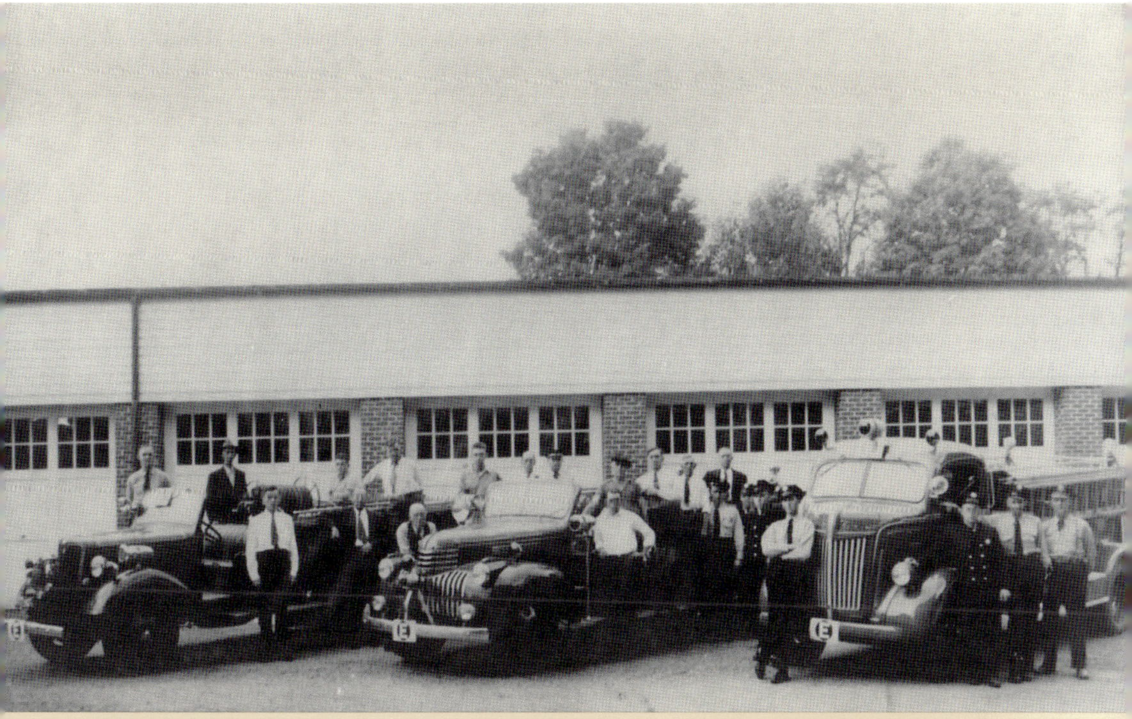

The Blacksburg fire department began with a hand-pulled 1892 American LaFrance Ladder Wagon in 1922. A number of serious fires resulted in the need for more powerful equipment, so pumpers and other trucks were bought in the 1940s. Unit 1, in the center, is a focal point of today's Blacksburg Fire Department Museum. (TOB.)

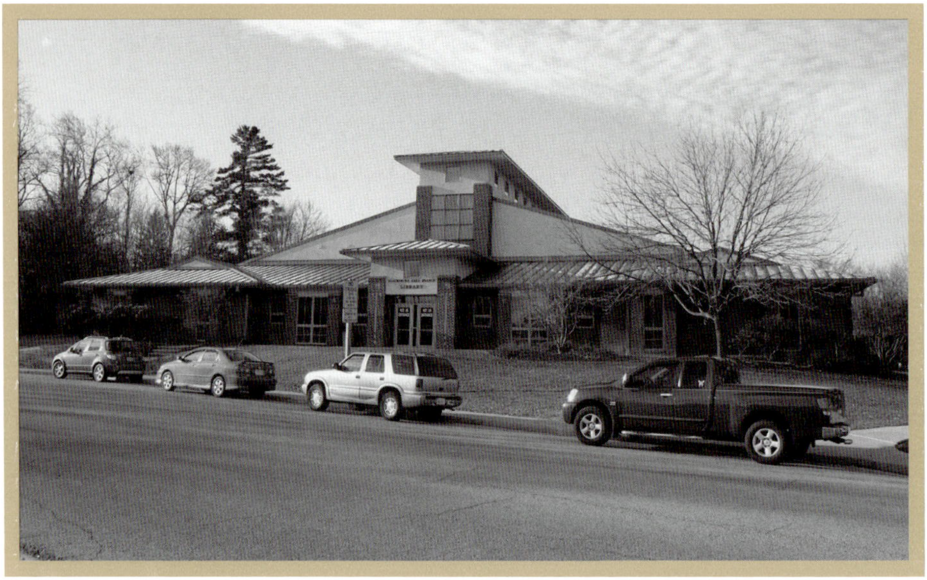

After a wait of nearly 50 years, Blacksburg welcomed railroad service in 1904, connecting the town through the coal mines at Merrimac to the town of Cambria, nine miles and a dangerous, curvy mountain road away. The train was called the "Huckleberry" for the low-bush blueberries growing along its tracks. The first depot was located where Blacksburg's library is today. The old rail bed follows today's Huckleberry Trail from the library parking lot through Merrimac to the New River Valley Mall. (DLA.)

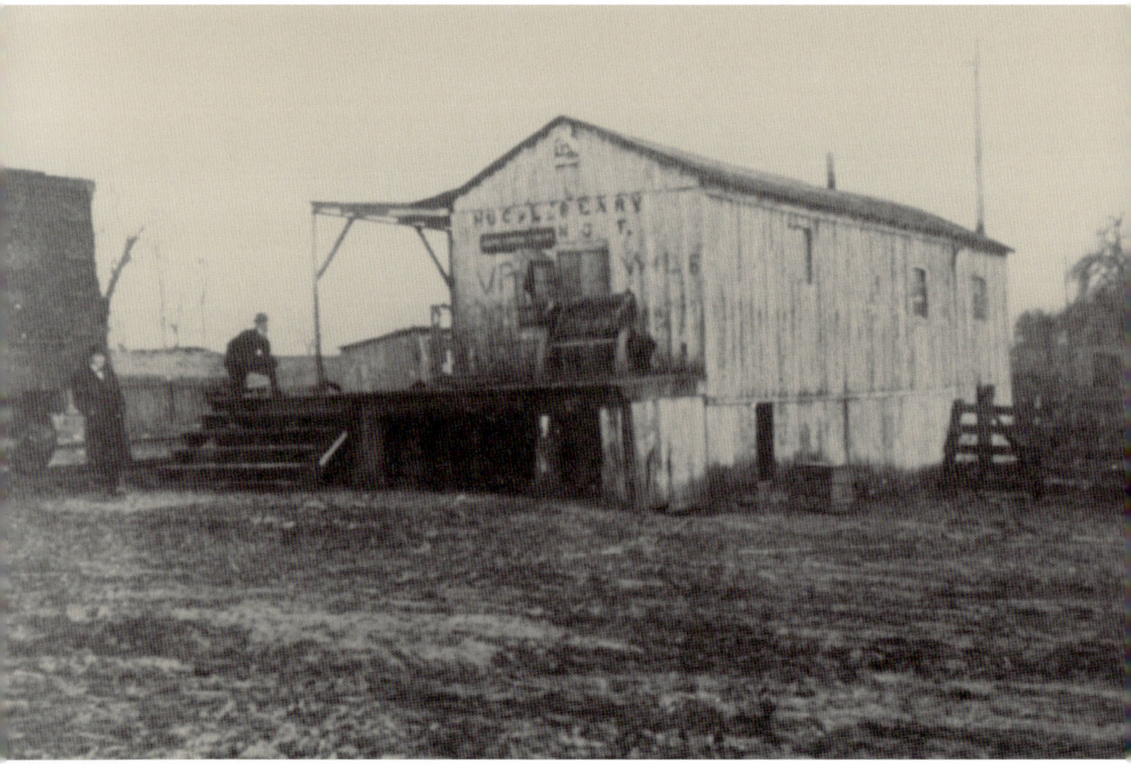

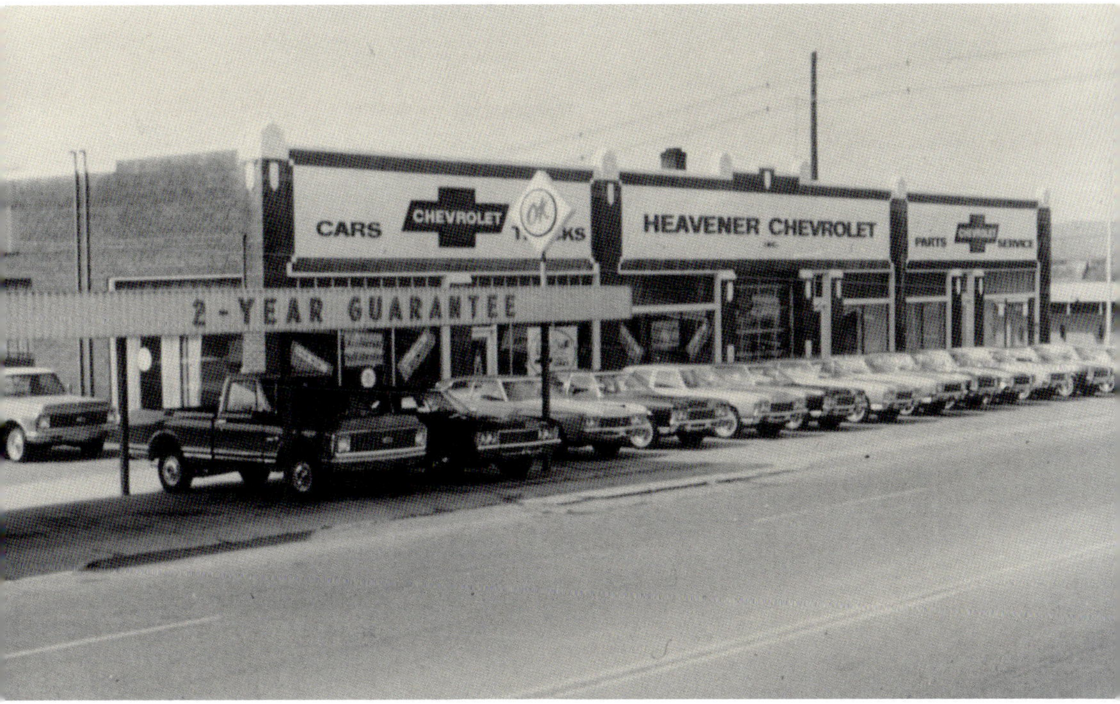

The Blacksburg Motor Company was constructed in 1924 in the Art Deco style. It would go on to house Heavener Chevrolet and Doc Roberts Tire Company and was purchased by the Town of Blacksburg in 2007. The structure, listed in the National Register of Historic Places, was renovated into a LEED Platinum building. Although it retained its original name, it is now home to the town's Planning and Building Department and its Engineering and GIS Department. (DLA.)

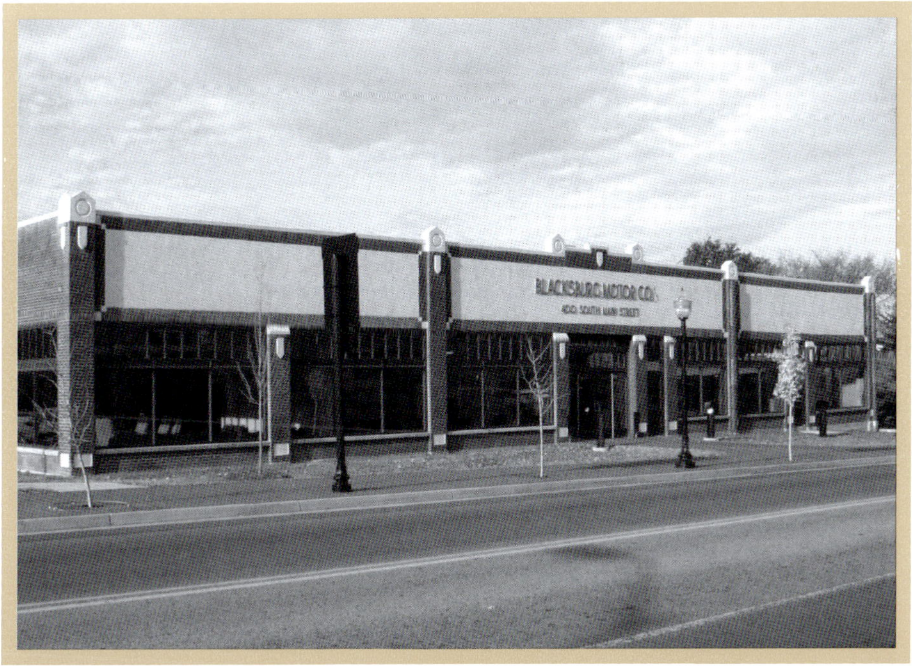

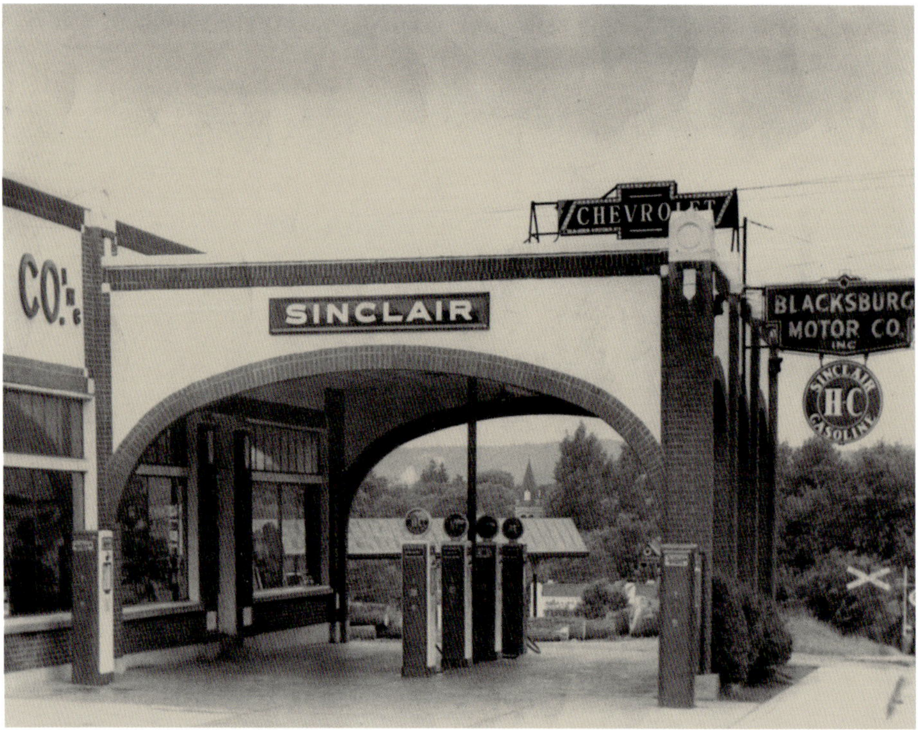

While originally built as a car dealership, the Blacksburg Motor Company boasted many features of convenience, including these gas pumps, under a canopy to protect them from weather. In the 1920s, the dealership also boasted a ladies' restroom, a rare luxury in the 1920s. The remnants of the canopy can still be seen in the different brick pattern on the columns of the facade. (TOB.)

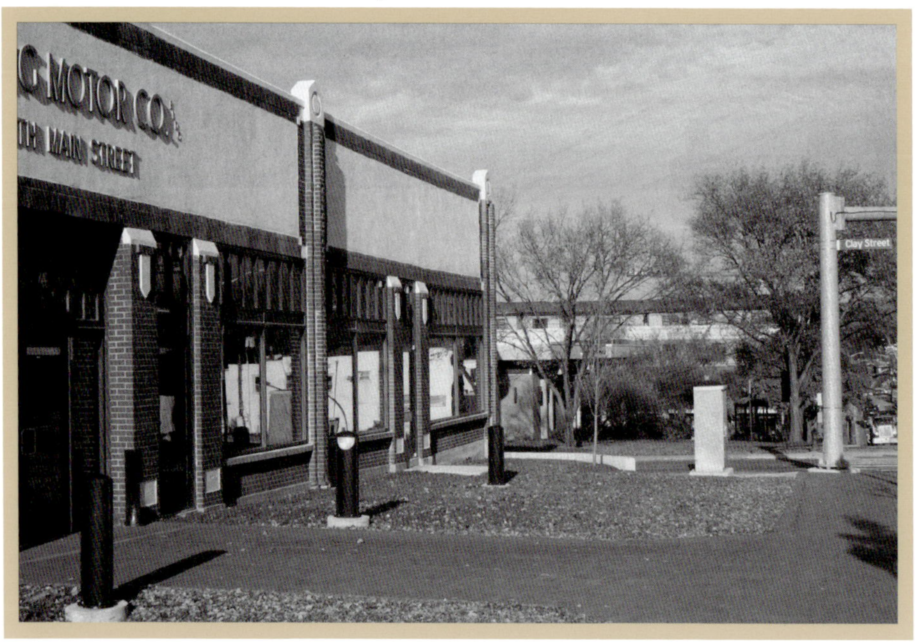

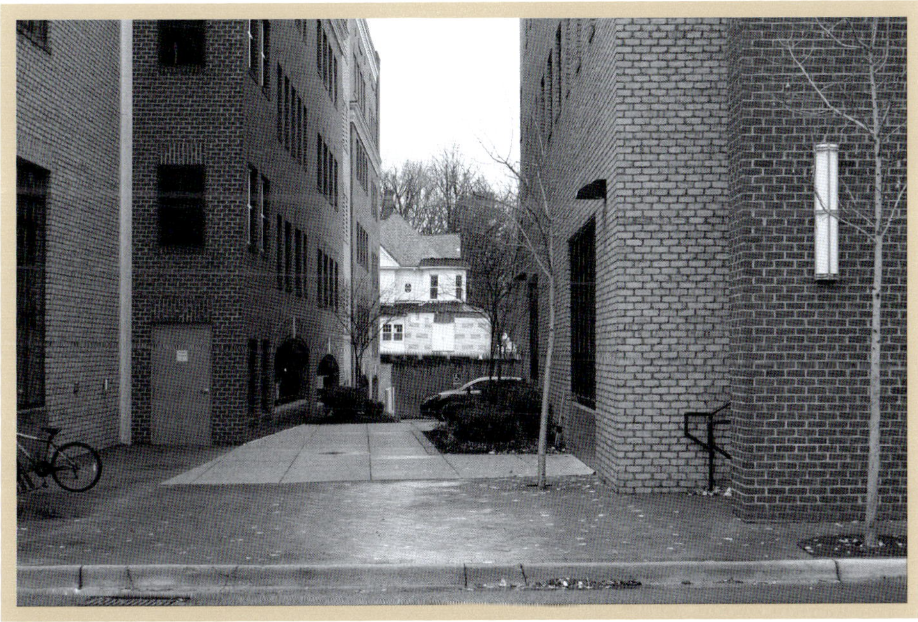

Alexander Black, grandnephew of town namesake William Black, built this Queen Anne Victorian house on Main Street in 1897 at a cost of $3,500. The home later became a succession of funeral homes before it was purchased by the Town of Blacksburg to be restored as the Blacksburg Museum and Cultural Center. The house was moved across the street to its current location on Draper Road in 2002 to make way for the Kent Square complex. (JK.)

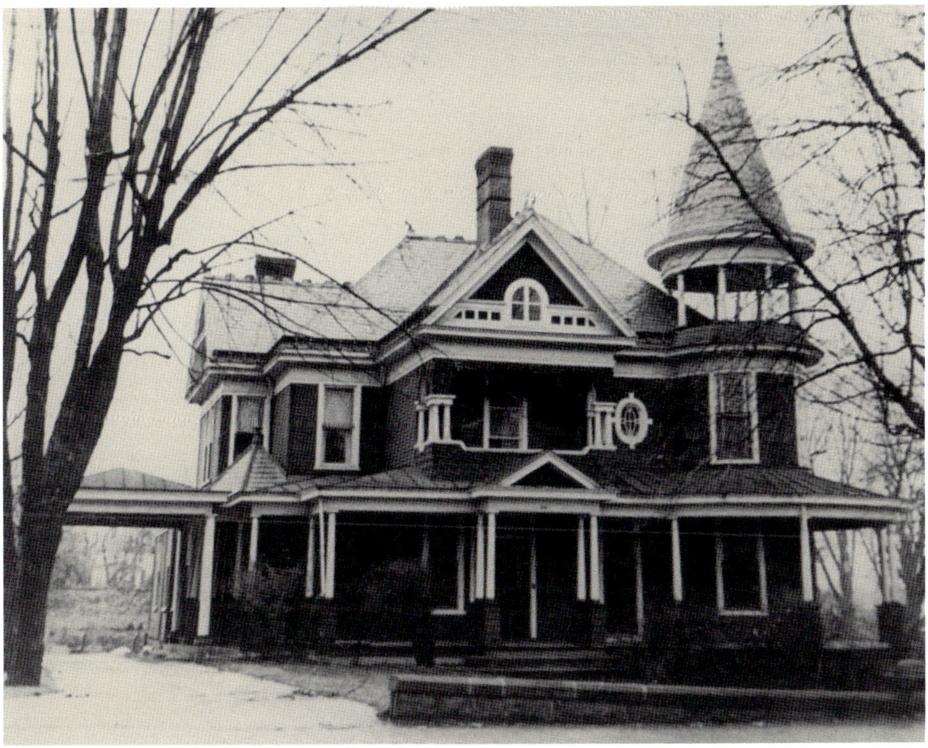

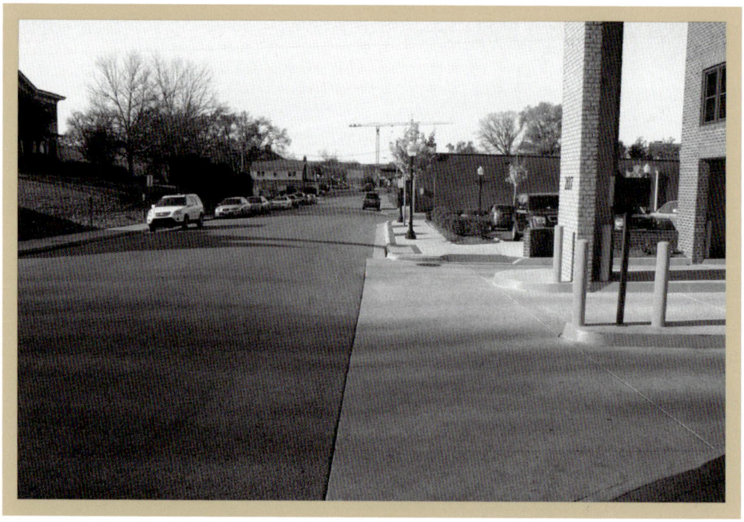

This springhouse sat directly behind the Alexander Black House and is one of several springs in the original Sixteen Squares of Blacksburg, all of which converge to feed Strouble's Creek. The spring was located in what is now the small parking lot behind Starbuck's Coffee. Standing in that parking lot, one can still hear the spring flowing in the underground storm drain. (DLA.)

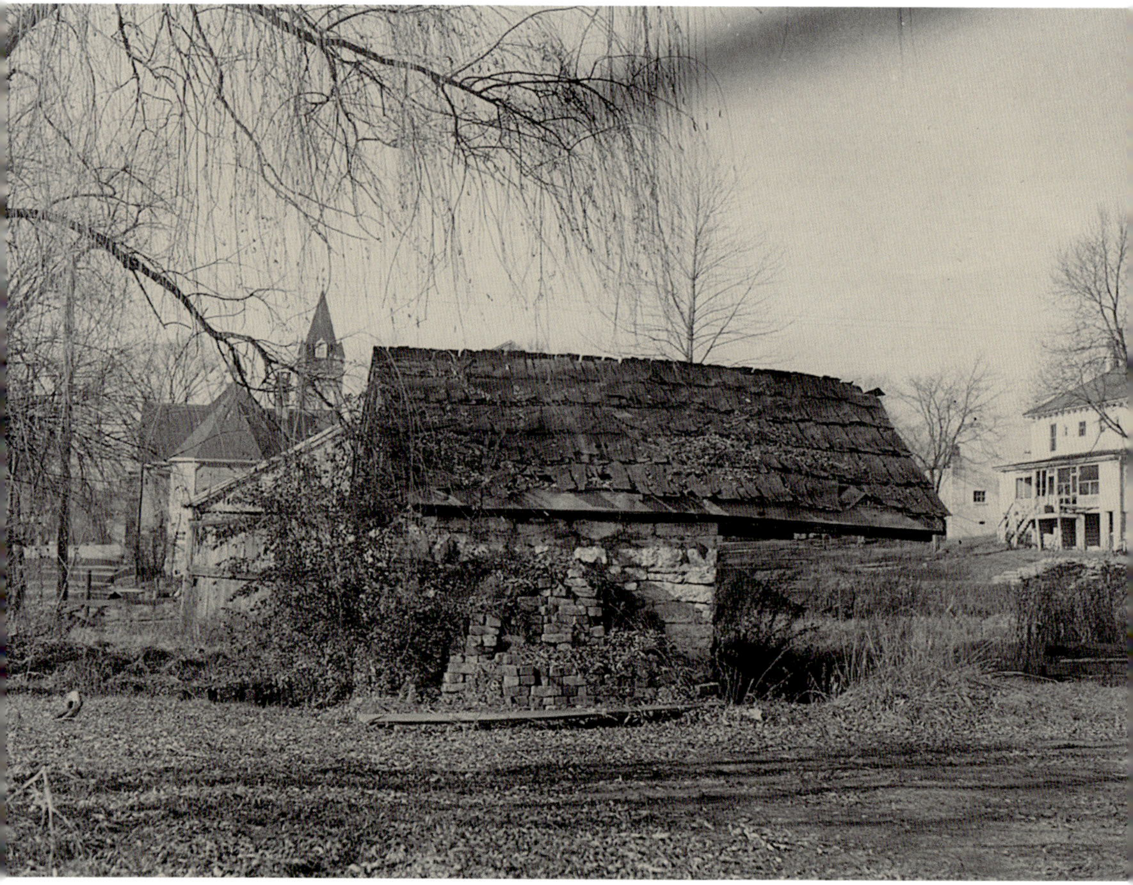

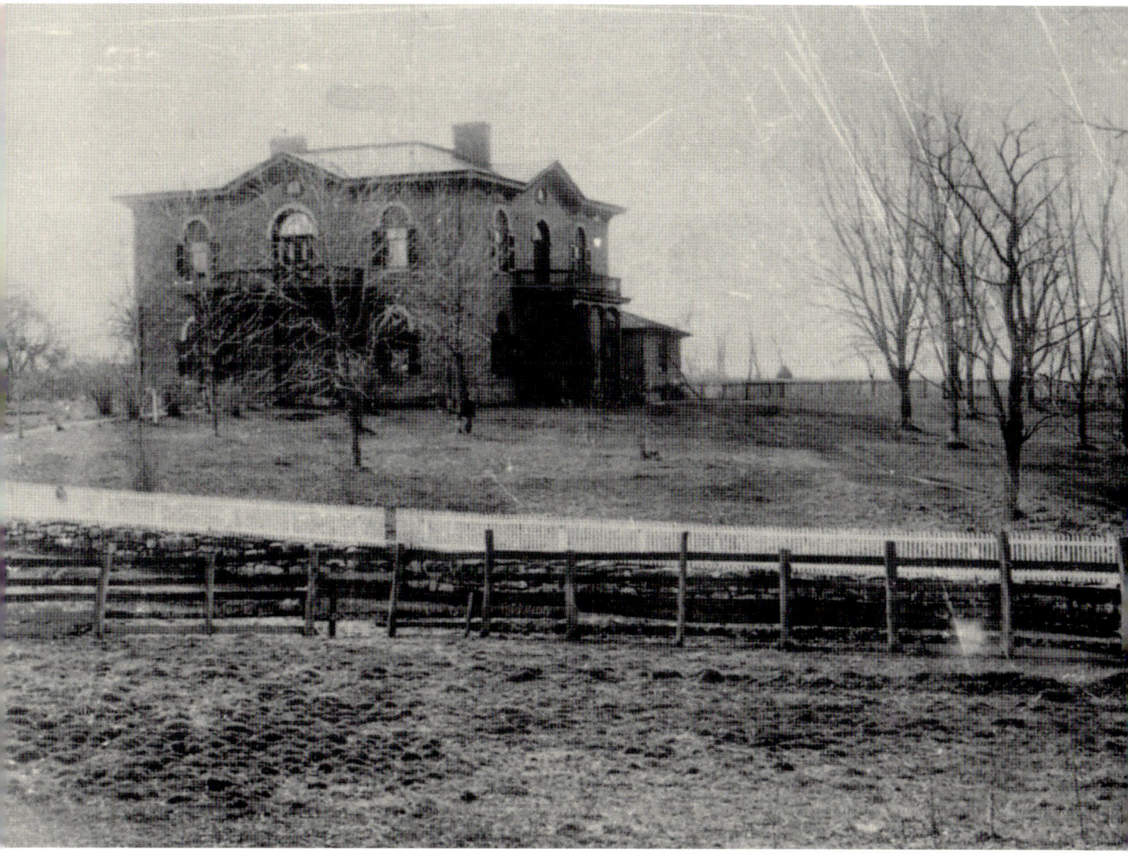

The Thomas-Conner House on Draper Road was built by William H. Thomas for $10,000 as a wedding gift for his daughter Mary in 1878. The Italianate-style architecture is expressed in the large eave brackets, low-pitched roof, and arched windows. Mary and John Conner moved into the house in 1882. The house remained in the family until 1972. Today, it is owned by the Town of Blacksburg and houses the Virginia Tech Center for Public Administration and Policy. (JK.)

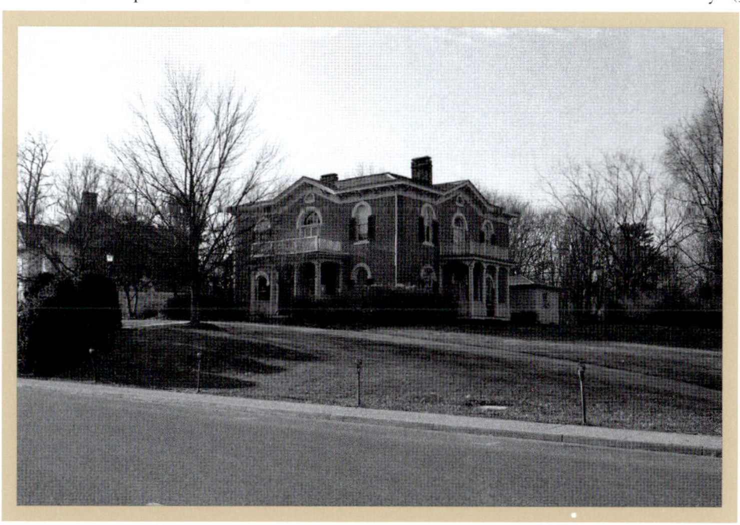

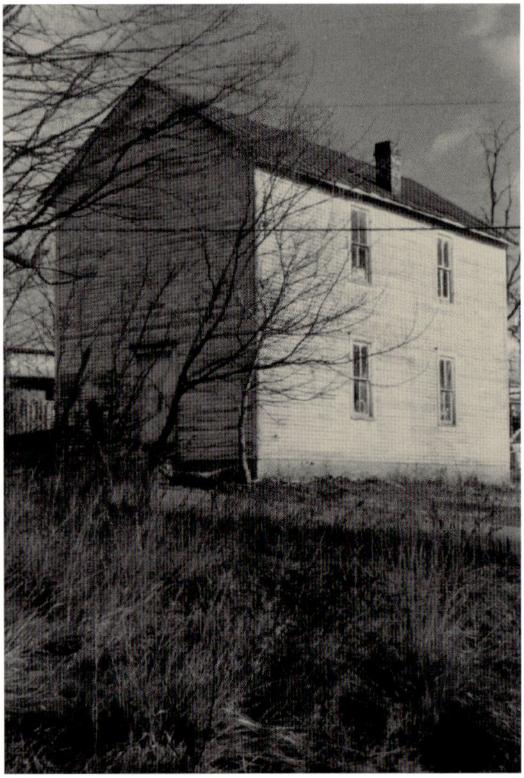

The St. Luke and Odd Fellows Hall (1905) was a meeting space for two black fraternal organizations. The structure was the center of New Town, a segregated community of about 20 homes that lined Gilbert Street and an alley off Main Street. The neighborhood was partially wiped out when Price's Fork Road was extended to Main Street, and further development gradually consumed the remaining houses. The restored hall houses a museum of Blacksburg's African American history. (TOB.)

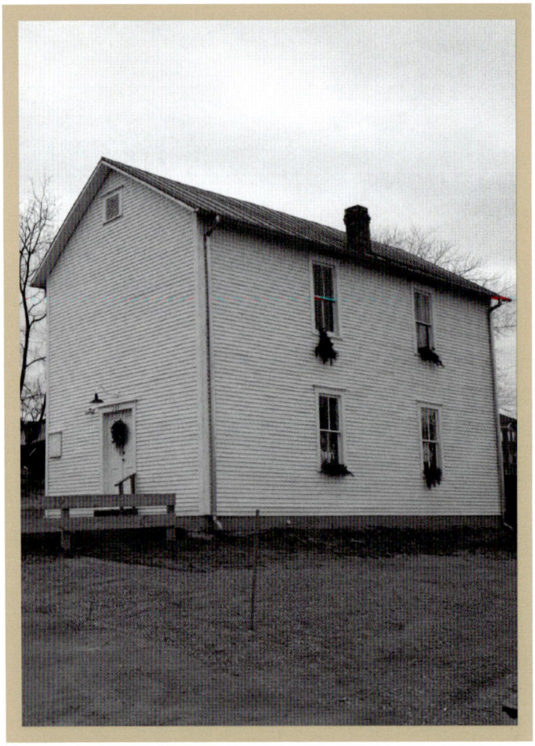

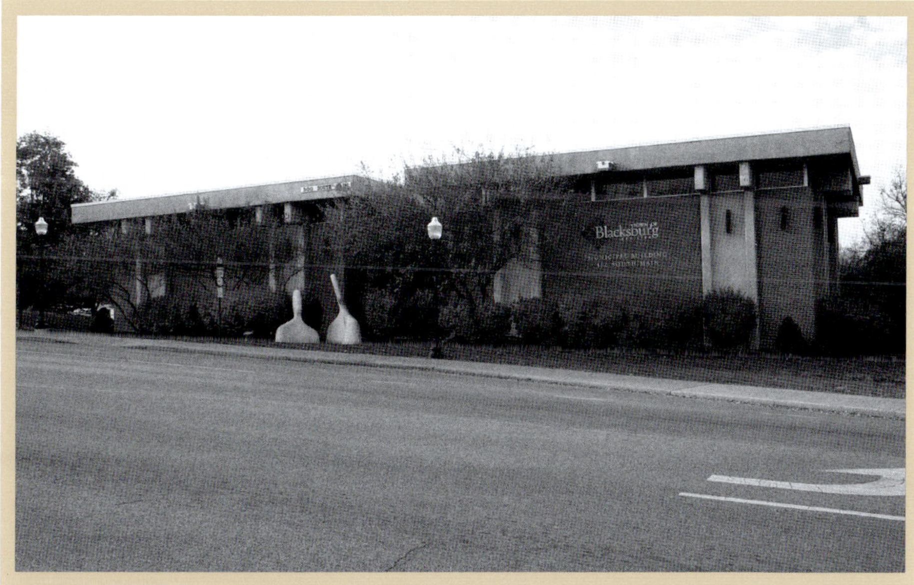

Norfolk & Western Railway purchased the Virginia Anthracite Coal and Railway Company in 1911. A new depot closer to Main Street was built for the Blacksburg branch, fares were reduced, and service improved. Passenger train service to Blacksburg ended in 1958, and freight service ended in 1966. The depot was removed in 1967. Blacksburg's Municipal Building was constructed on the same site in 1969 and remains home to the town's administrative offices and town council chambers. (DLA.)

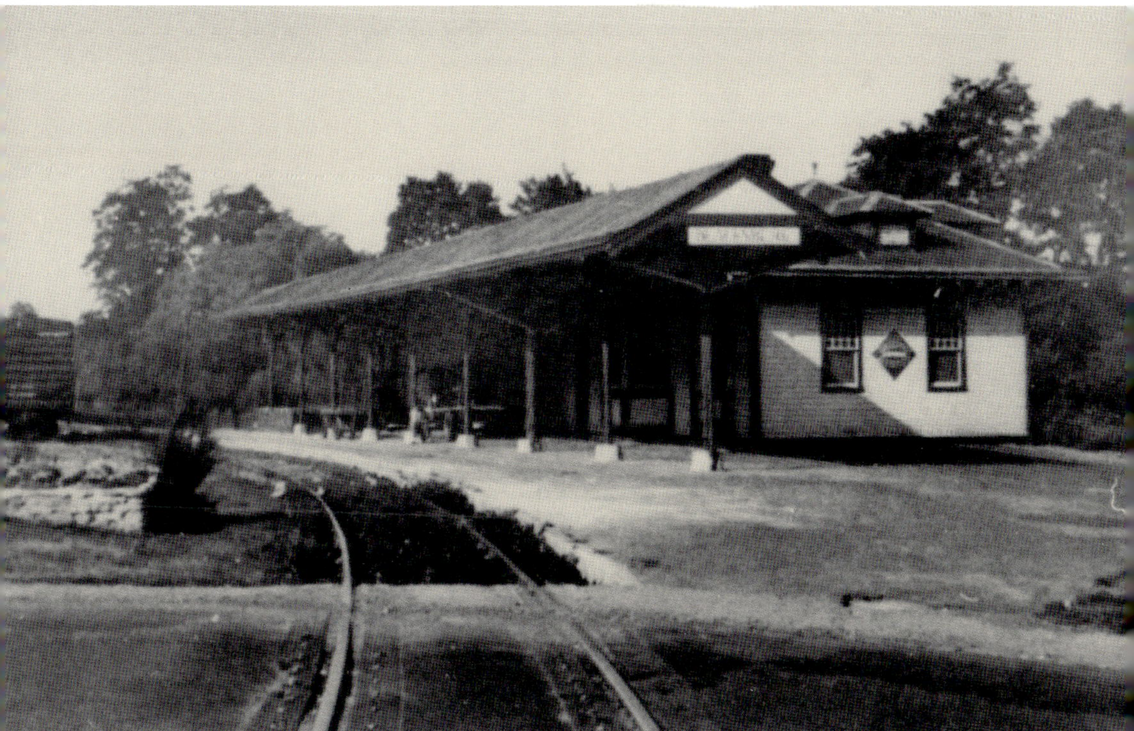

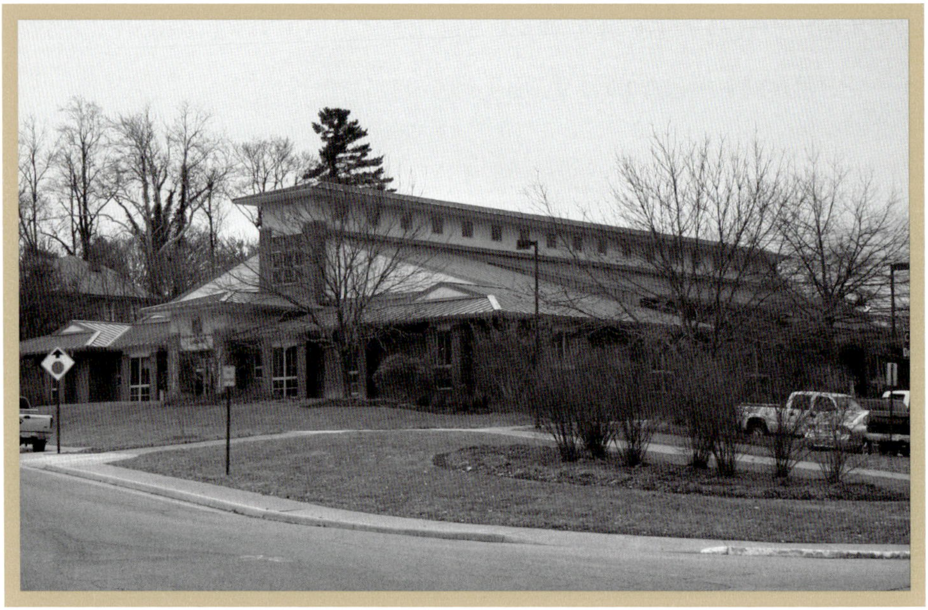

The Blacksburg Lumber Company was constructed on Draper Road at the site of the first Huckleberry Railway depot. The Blacksburg branch of the Montgomery Regional Library moved into the building in 1980. A new library building was completed on the site in 1986, with a design evoking the memory of the train depot once inhabiting the site. (DLA.)

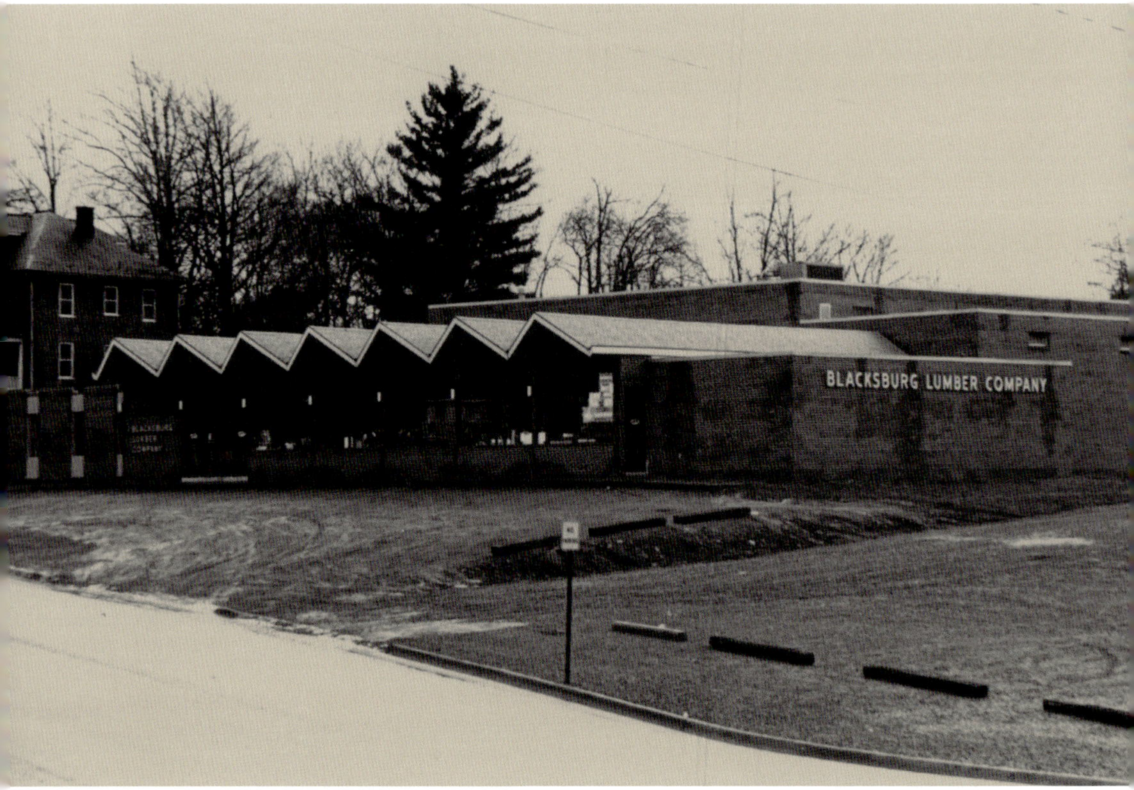

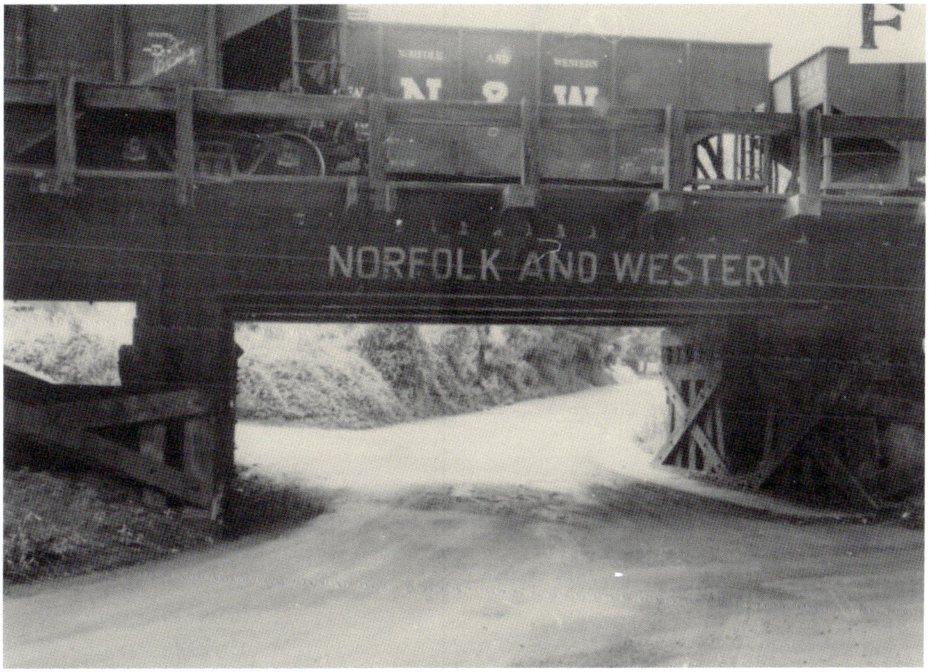

Virginia Anthracite Coal and Railway Company built the railroad to connect the coal mines at Merrimac to the main Norfolk & Western Railway line at Cambria and later continued the line through to Blacksburg. The train was a popular way for Virginia Tech students and residents to travel to Christiansburg, Roanoke, and beyond. A trestle at Clay Street and Draper Road bridged a low area marking the streambed of one of Strouble's Creek tributaries and connecting the railroad to Main Street. (JK.)

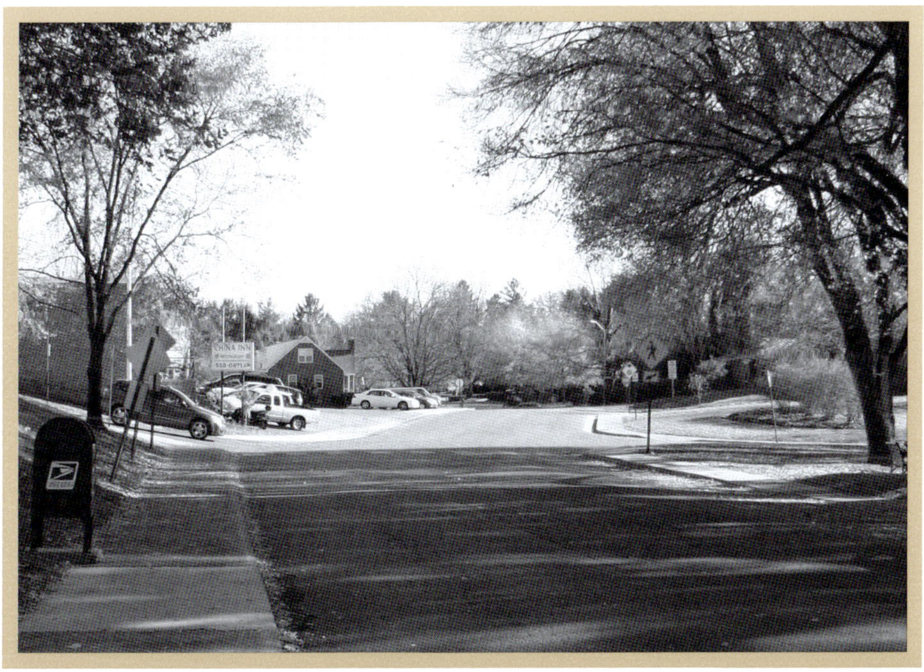

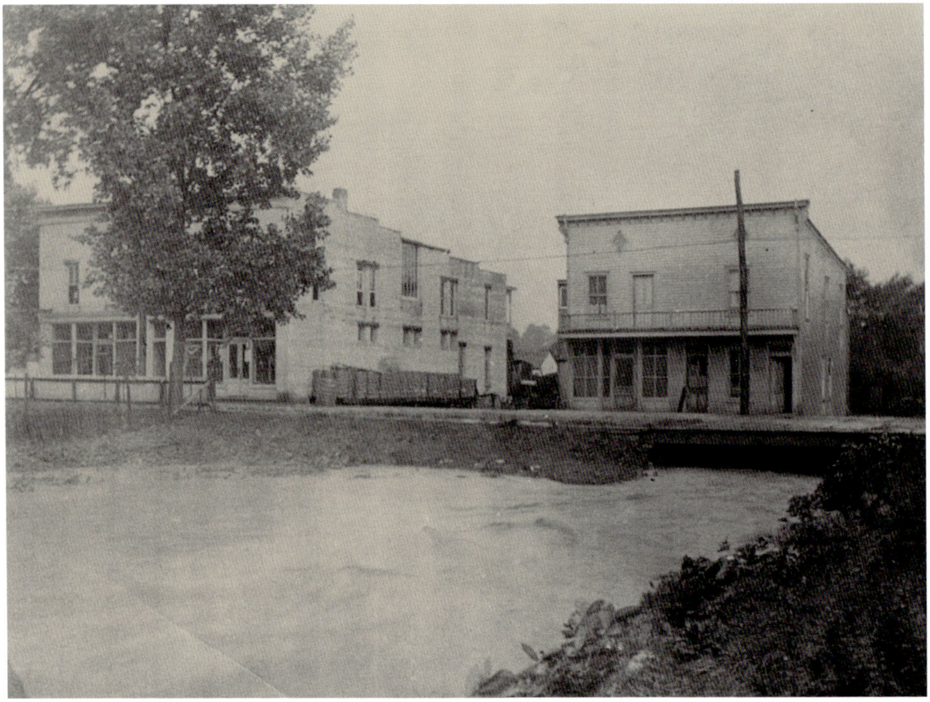

Blacksburg has a number of springs and creeks within its boundaries that attracted early settlers. Later, the water became a source of disease and, often, flooding. As the town developed, many of the creeks were routed under buildings and parking lots, worsening the flooding. The meandering sidewalk in the parking lot behind the buildings on North Main Street at the College Avenue intersection acknowledge the stream beneath. (DLA.)

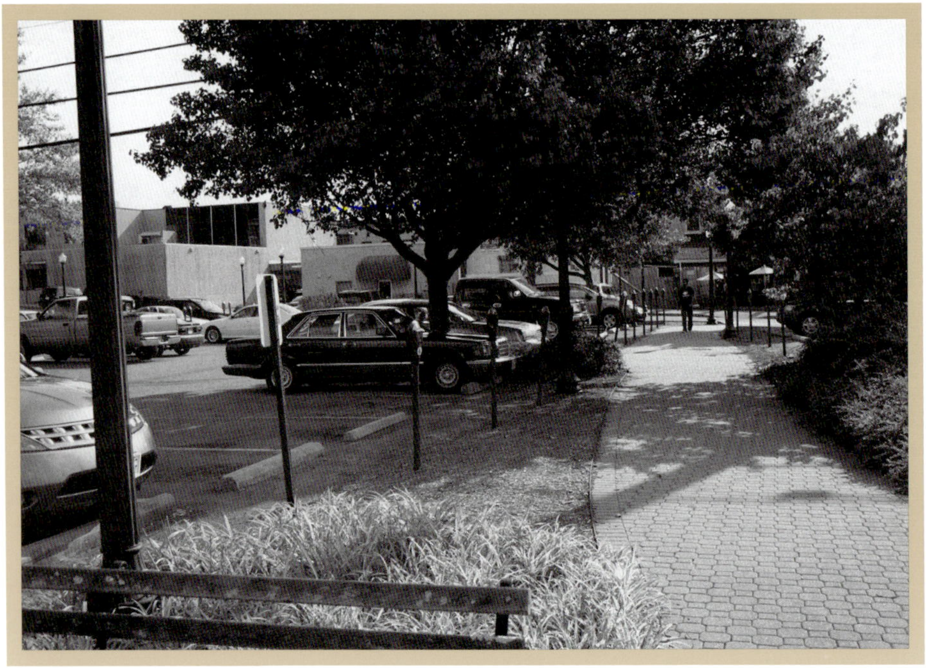

CHAPTER 3

Worship and Education

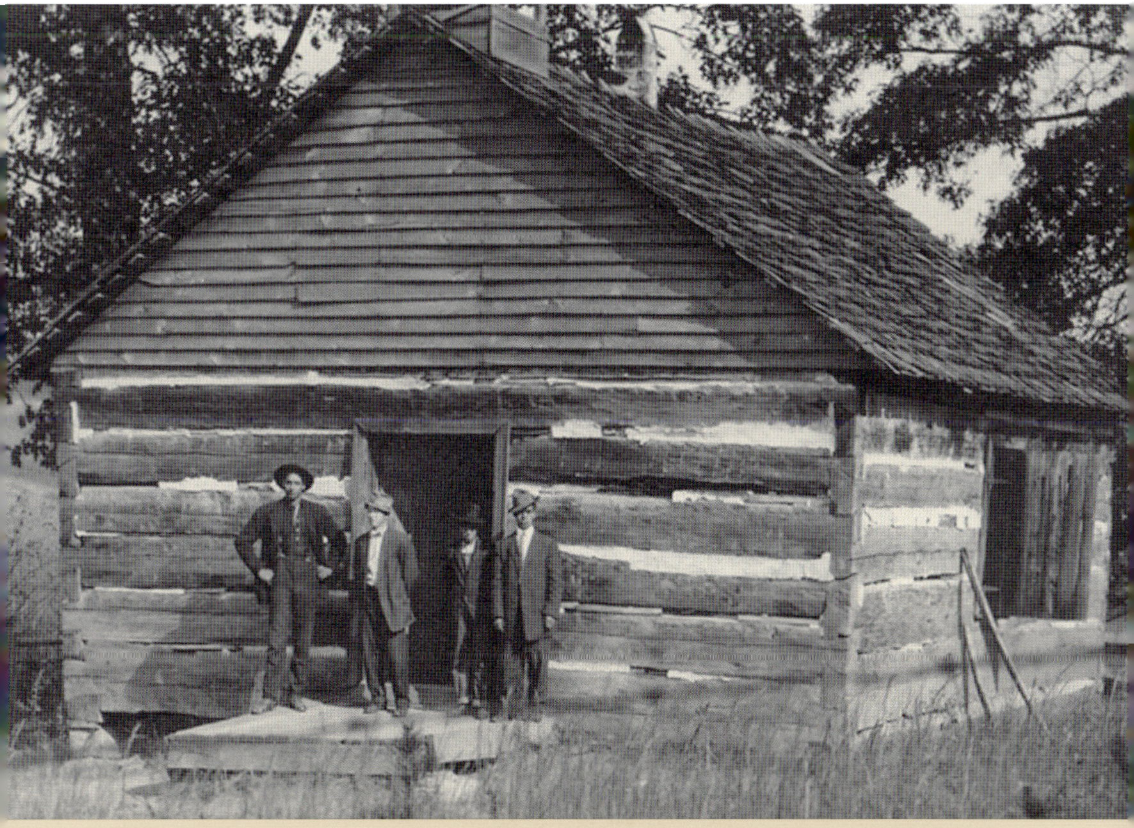

A handwritten note on this photograph states "Negro Church at Blacksburg." Enslaved African Americans were not allowed to gather without white supervision, even to worship, because whites feared insurrection. St. Paul AME on Penn Street was formed before the Civil War, and First Baptist Church on Clay Street was formed soon after. Both continue as vibrant congregations in the community. (TOB.)

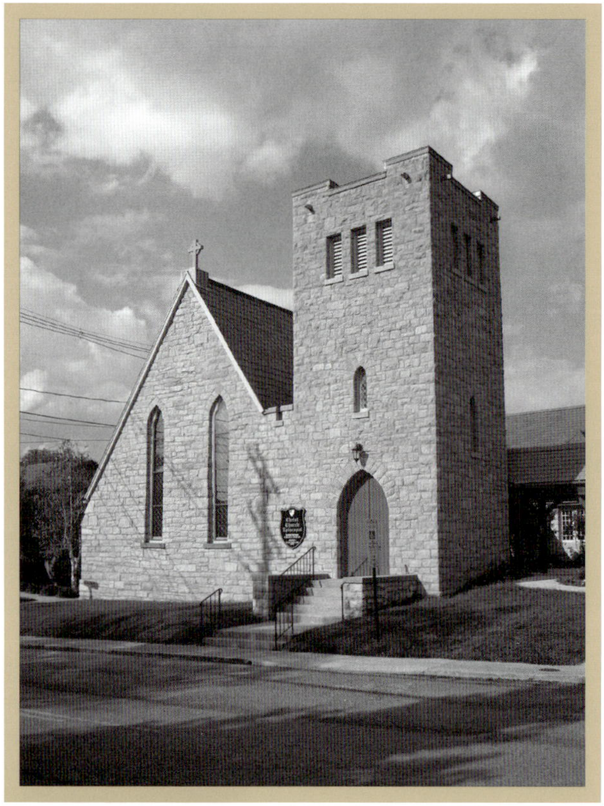

The main sanctuary of Christ Episcopal Church at Church and Jackson Streets was built of local limestone in 1874. The bell tower was built in 1934, followed by the parish house in 1942, an educational wing in 1972, and a parish hall completed in 1990. The church has recently undergone a $450,000 restoration to preserve the historic building, one of the oldest continuously used churches in Blacksburg. (DLA.)

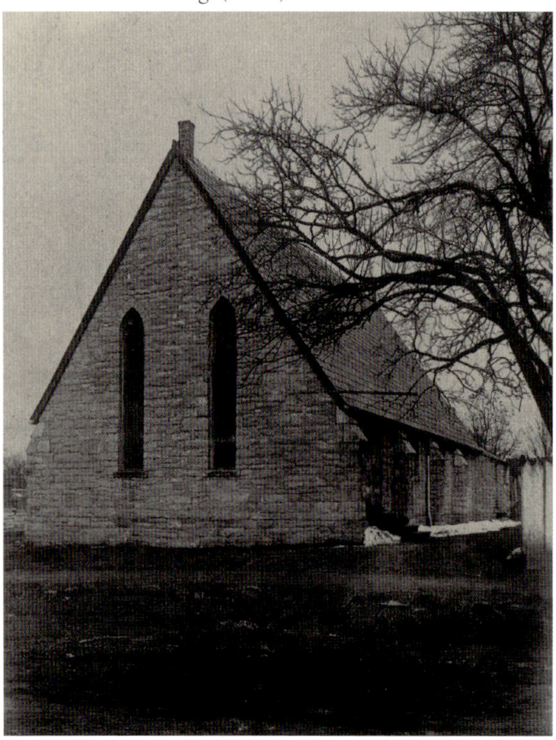

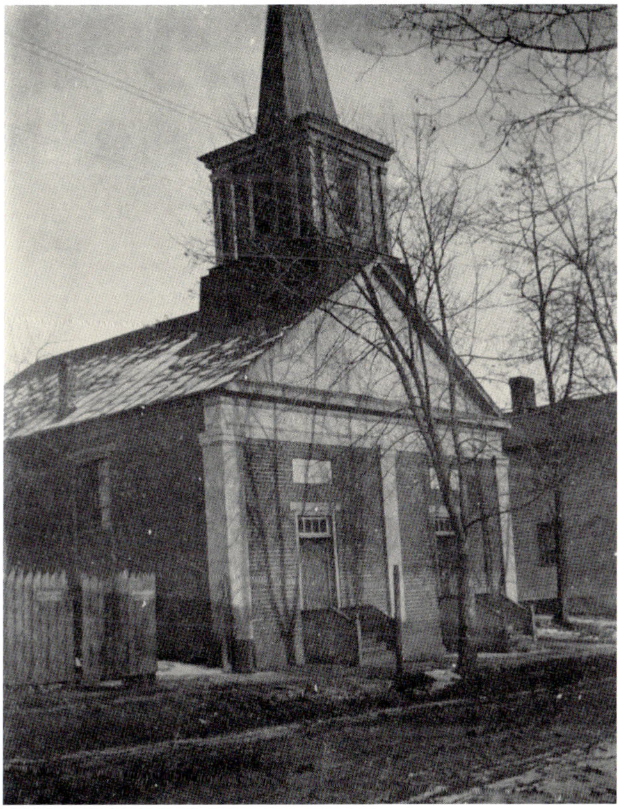

The Blacksburg Presbyterian Church was established in 1832 by members of the Christiansburg Presbyterian Church. The first brick church building was constructed on Main Street in 1847 and is currently home to the Cabo Fish Taco restaurant. A new Presbyterian church was built on Roanoke Street in 1904 and is now the First Church of God. Blacksburg Presbyterian Church moved to a new building at Church and Eakin Streets in 1955. (DLA.)

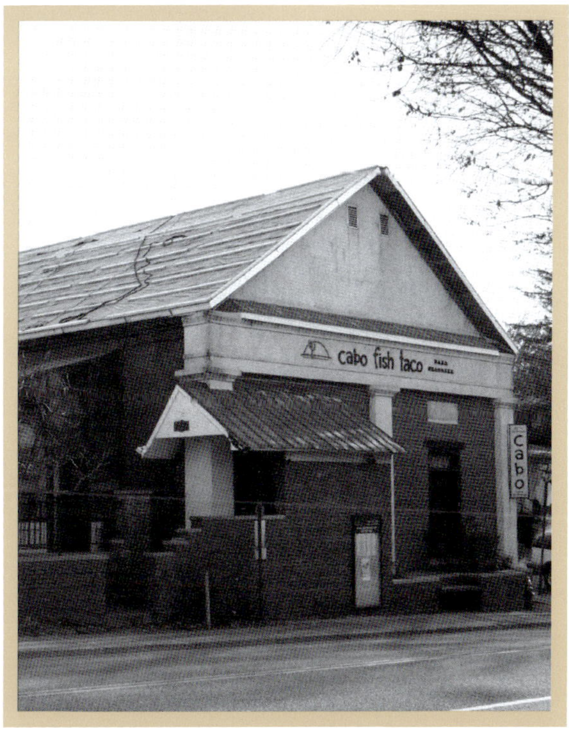

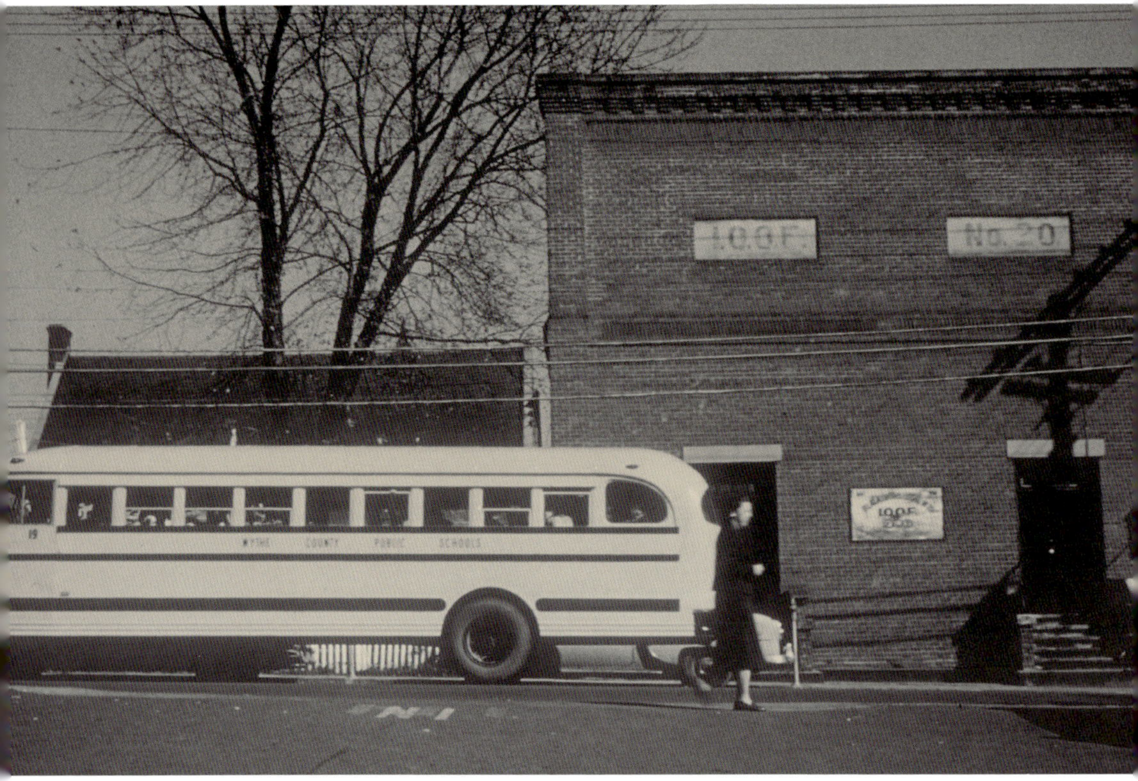

The old Presbyterian church building on Main Street was used for a number of years by Blacksburg's chapter of the Independent Order of Odd Fellows before becoming a series of restaurants. The Blacksburg Transit bus shown in the modern photograph is a common sight around town, providing transportation for students and townspeople. Bus service began in 1983 with six buses and has since expanded to 44. Some door-to-door service has been added to its traditional fixed routes. (TOB.)

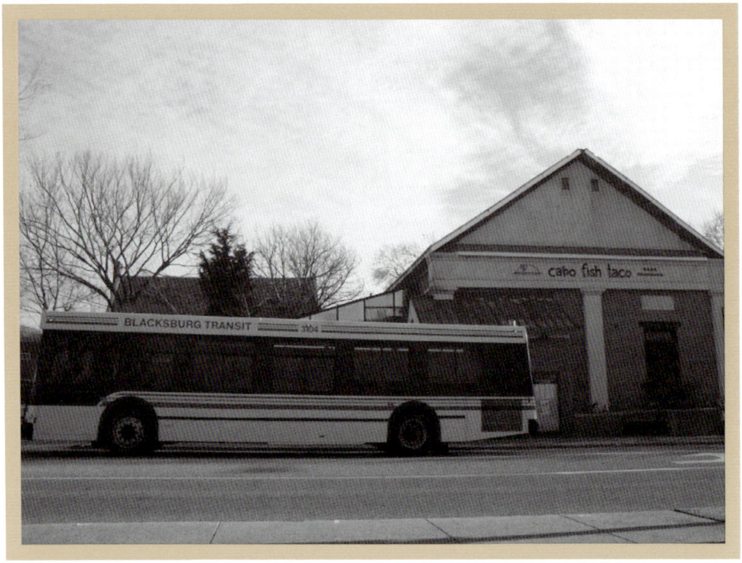

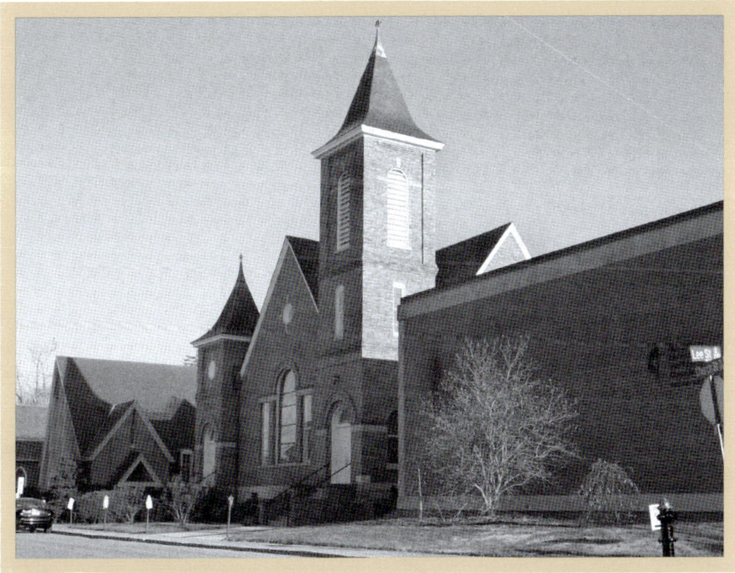

Lot 40 of Blacksburg's original Sixteen Squares was assigned to the Methodists for the construction of a church. The 1840 building shown below was the third church constructed on the site. Following continued church growth, the Whisner Building was constructed in 1905. As Blacksburg United Methodist Church continued to grow, the Whisner Building became the fellowship hall, with a new sanctuary and an education wing constructed in the 1950s and 1960s. (DLA.)

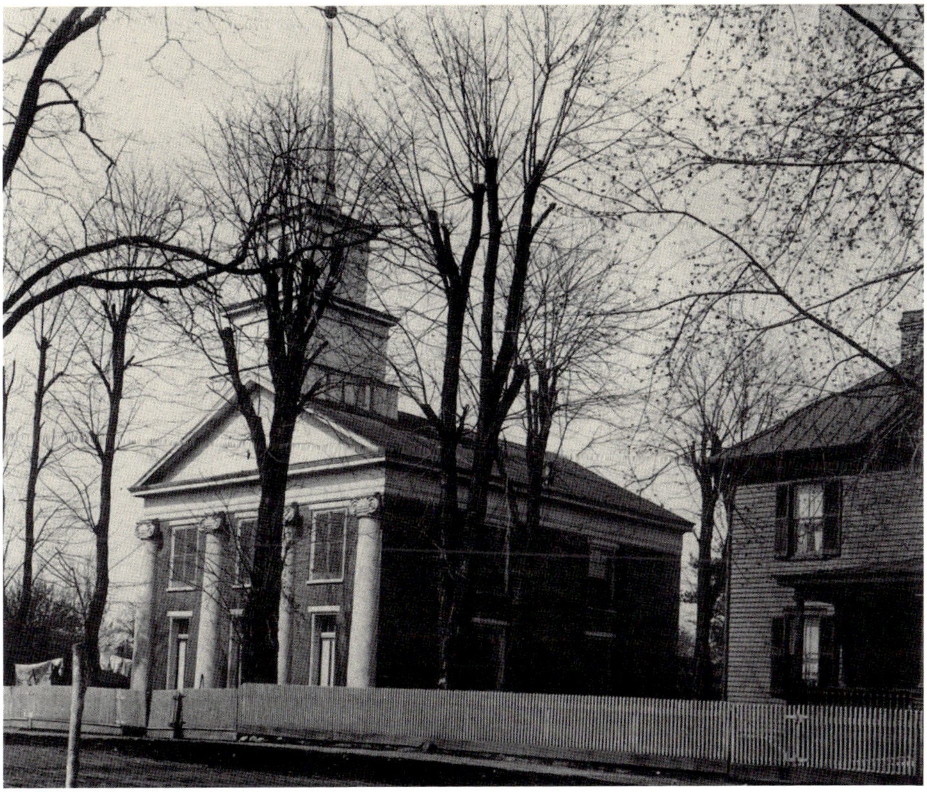

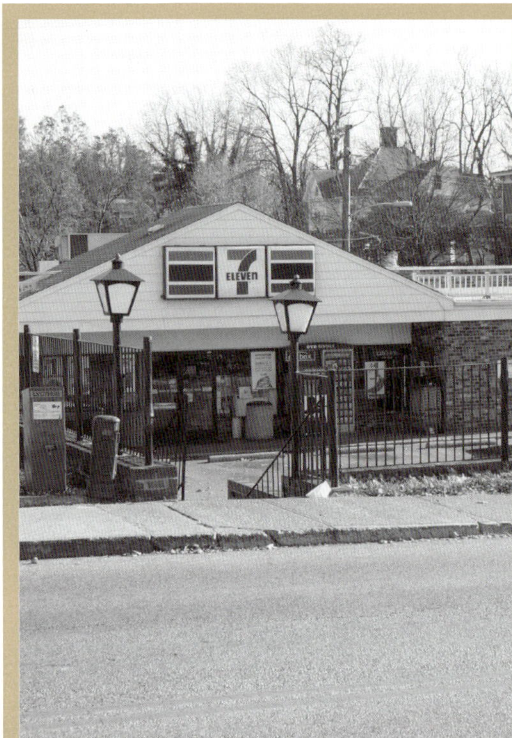

The third Blacksburg Baptist Church building was completed in 1903 at the corner of Roanoke Street and Draper Road. The church outgrew its location by 1944 and began planning to construct a new building: its current location on North Main Street, which was dedicated in 1953. The old building became the Church of God and subsequently burned in 1958. Today, the 7-11 convenience store occupies space in what was the church's basement. (DLA.)

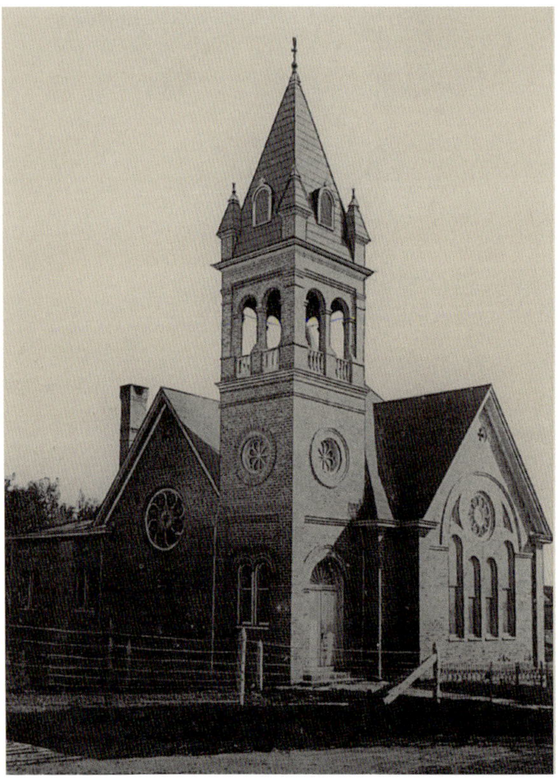

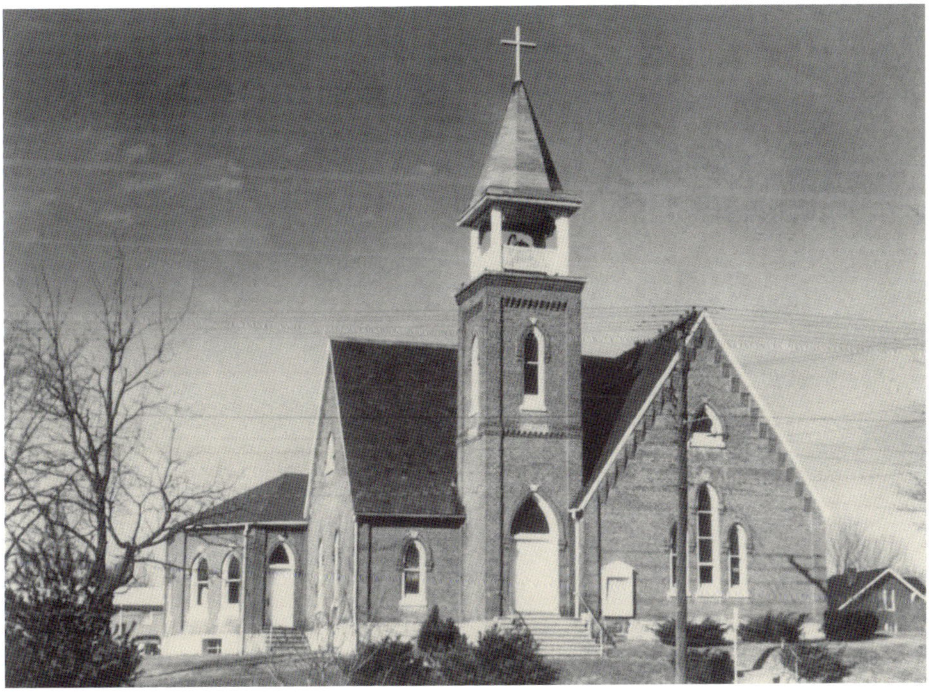

Luther Memorial Lutheran Church was completed in 1883 on Turner Street after a kiln on the grounds had fired 133,000 bricks. Eighty thousand were used to construct the building, and the rest were sold as a fundraiser. A new church was completed at Tom's Creek and Price's Fork Roads in 1972. The site of the old church is now occupied by McDonald's. Steps from the old church grounds are still visible between the McDonald's and the Sub Station II. (DLA.)

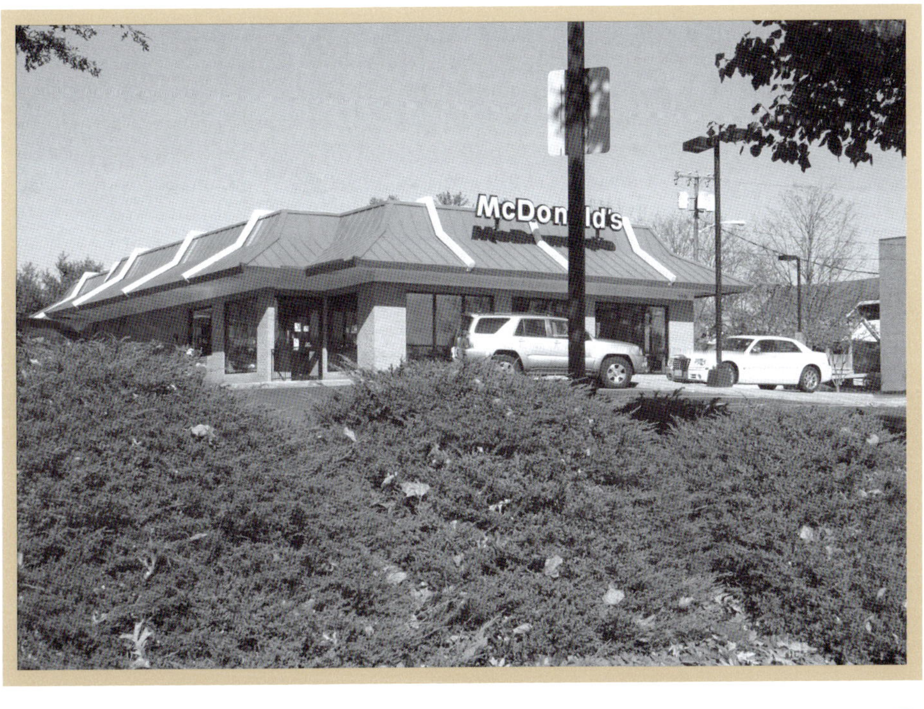

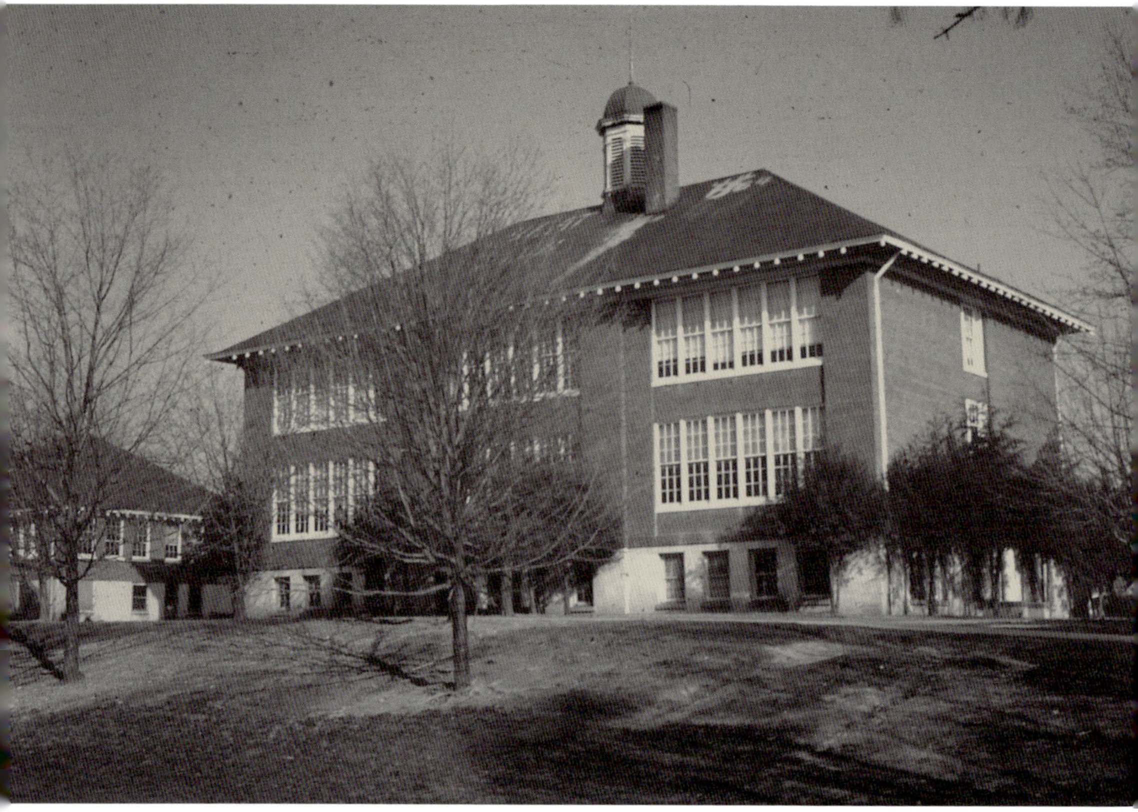

Blacksburg High School was built in 1916 in the center of town. The building to the left was constructed in 1921 to house agricultural and shop programs for Montgomery County schools. Nearby but not visible, Blacksburg Elementary School was built in 1934. All three buildings were sold to Virginia Tech at auction in 1965. The high school building is used as the Architecture Annex and was renovated after a 1997 fire. (JK.)

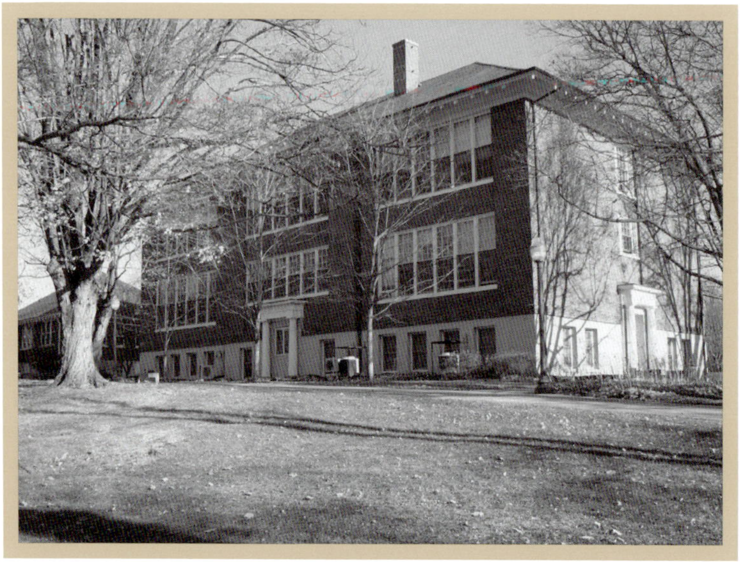

CHAPTER 4

THE TOWN EXPANDS

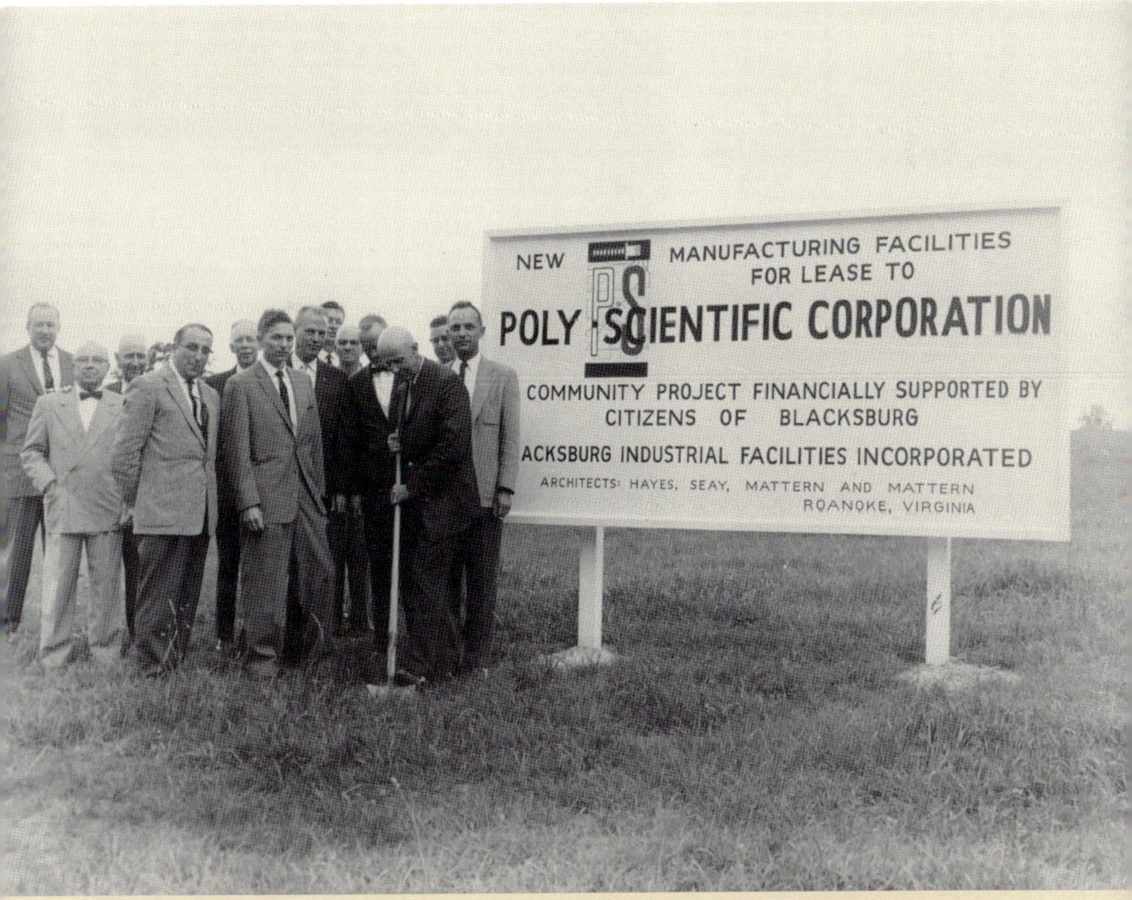

As Virginia Tech has expanded, Blacksburg's population has grown, driving commercial development on the outskirts of town. Manufacturing, engineering, and technology companies have populated the Blacksburg Industrial Park and Virginia Tech Corporate Research Center. Poly-Scientific, founded in Blacksburg in 1953 by James Pandapas, remains in Blacksburg as today's Moog Components Group and has expanded to additional sites throughout the years. (DLA.)

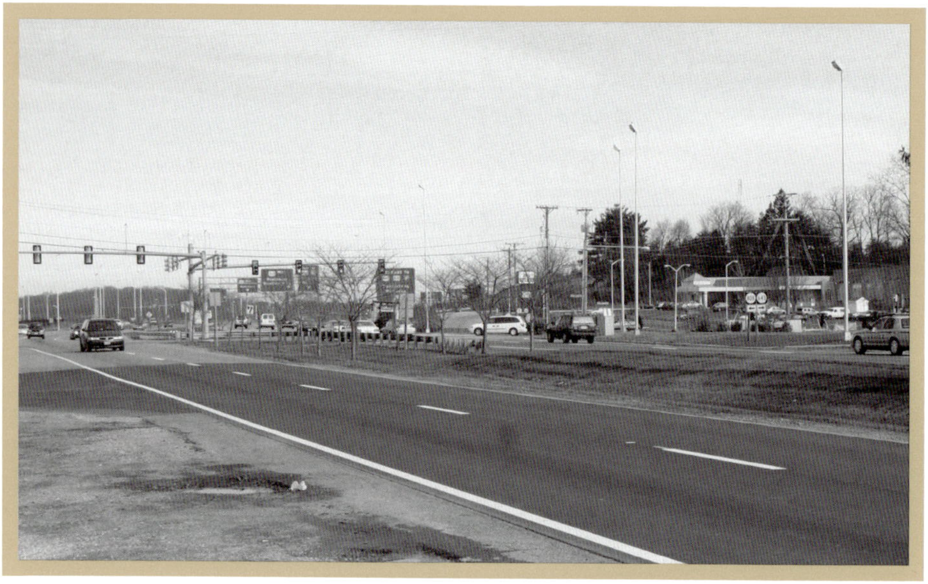

As automobiles became more reliable and affordable, traffic became a problem in Blacksburg. One attempt to alleviate this problem was the construction of the Route 460 bypass around town, which was completed in 1969, in time to connect to the new Interstate 81 at Christiansburg when it opened in 1971. With the continued growth of Virginia Tech, a bypass of the commercial strip that grew up around Route 460 between Blacksburg and Christiansburg was completed recently to further facilitate Blacksburg's connection to Interstate 81. (DLA.)

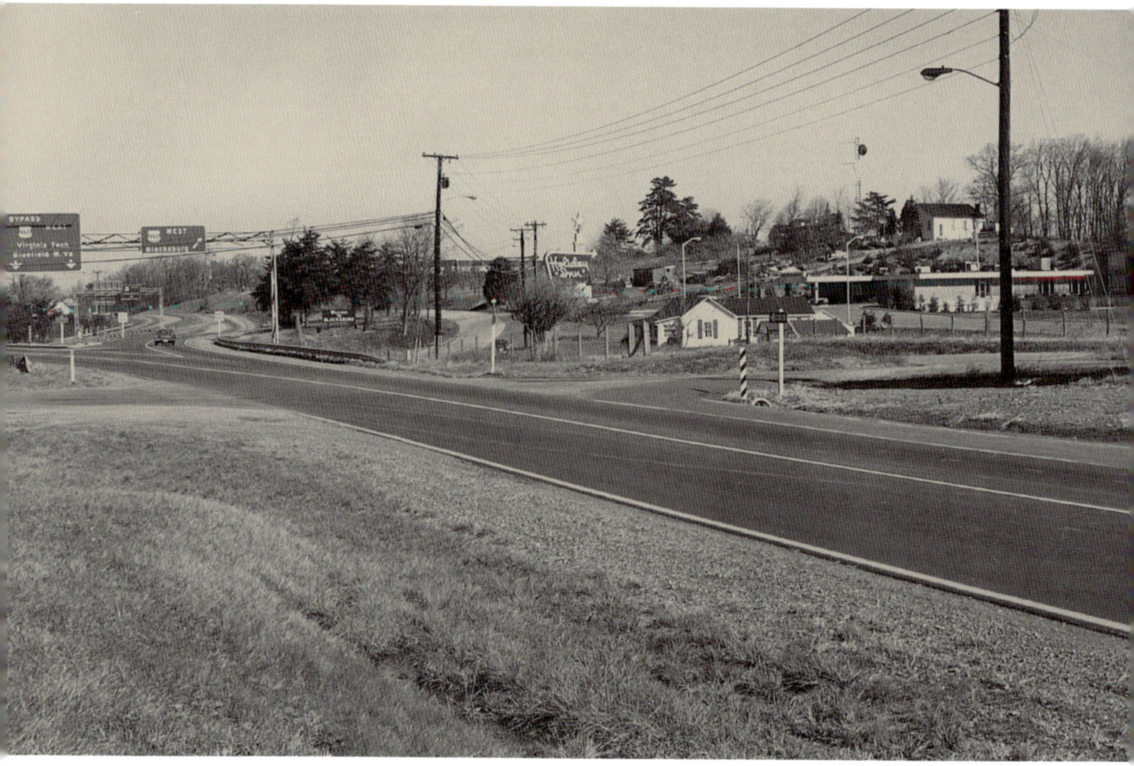

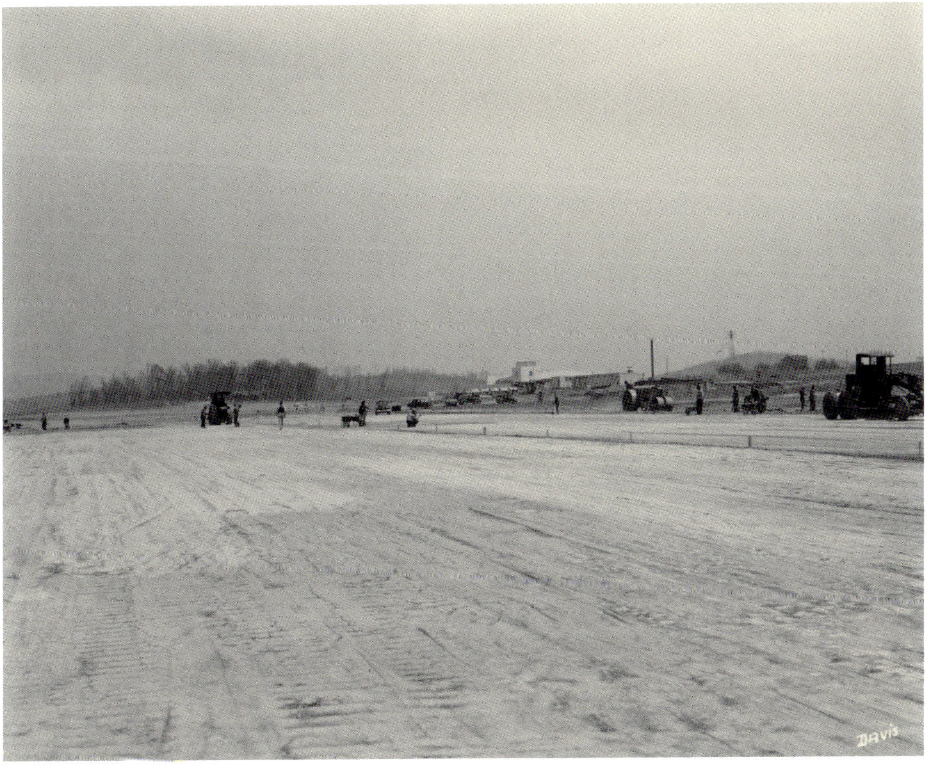

A 1,800-foot grass landing strip was built in Blacksburg in 1929 as one of Virginia's 35 emergency landing fields, and it became an airport in 1931. The grass landing strip was augmented with a 2,850-foot paved runway in 1941 for the Defense Department's Civilian Pilot Training Program. After years of flight training for Virginia Tech's Corps of Cadets, the Virginia Tech Montgomery Executive Airport has transformed into a community airport, serving corporate jets on its two 4,539-foot runways. (DLA.)

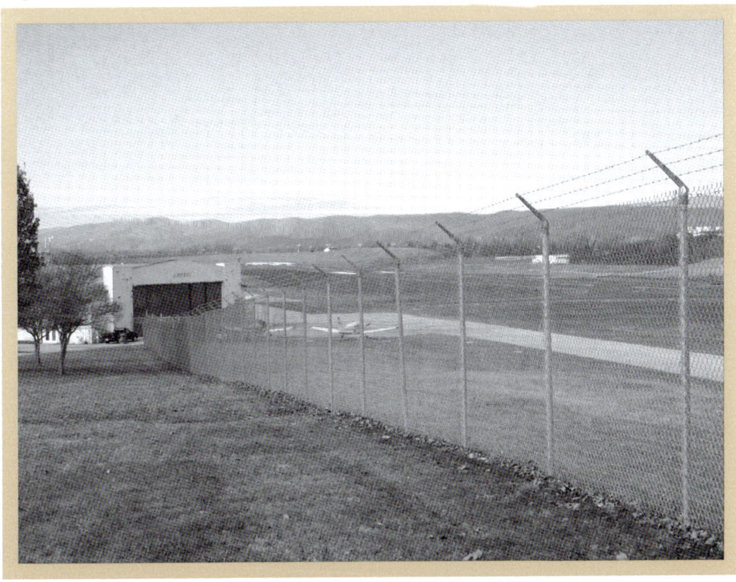

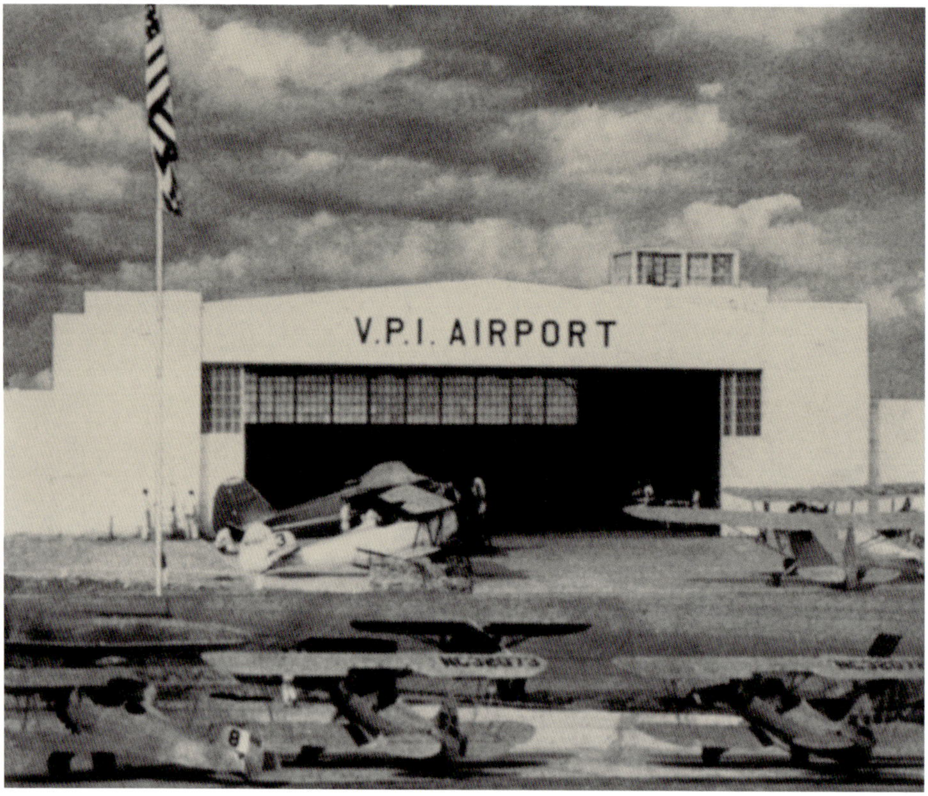

The hangar at the Virginia Tech airport was completed in 1940 as part of the Defense Department's Civilian Pilot Training Program, and 15 aircraft were purchased to train pilots and mechanics. The hangar remains in service today, but a new, modern terminal was added recently to serve the private and corporate jets that frequent the airport for business travel and Hokie football games. (DLA.)

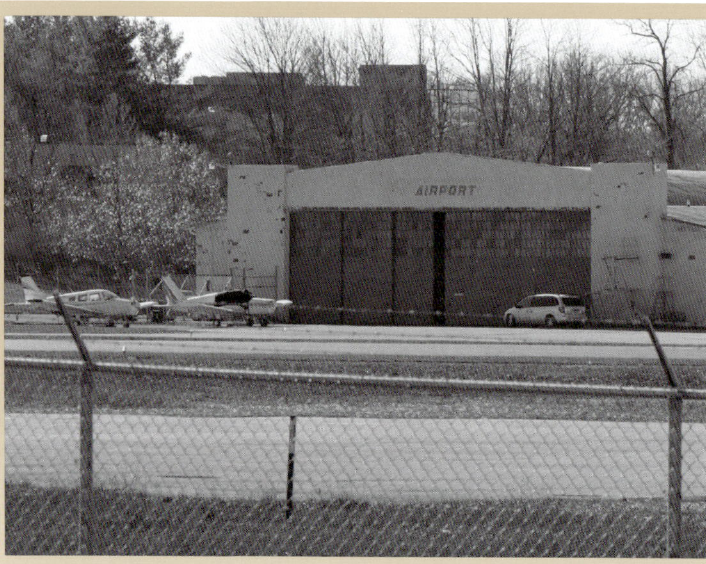

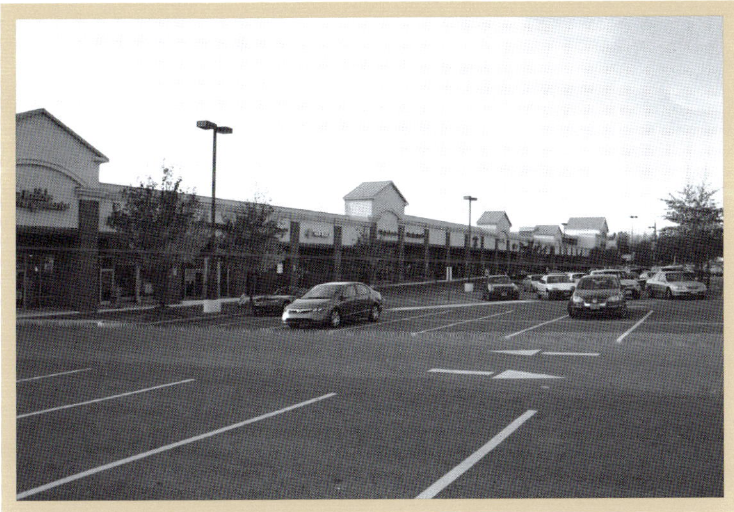

As Blacksburg grew, so did the need for larger stores for local shoppers. Gables Shopping Center opened on North Main Street in 1966, and within 10 years, it included Sears, A&P, and Leggett's. Gables Shopping Center recently underwent renovations to create a larger Kroger store to anchor the center, which also includes a number of smaller businesses. (DLA.)

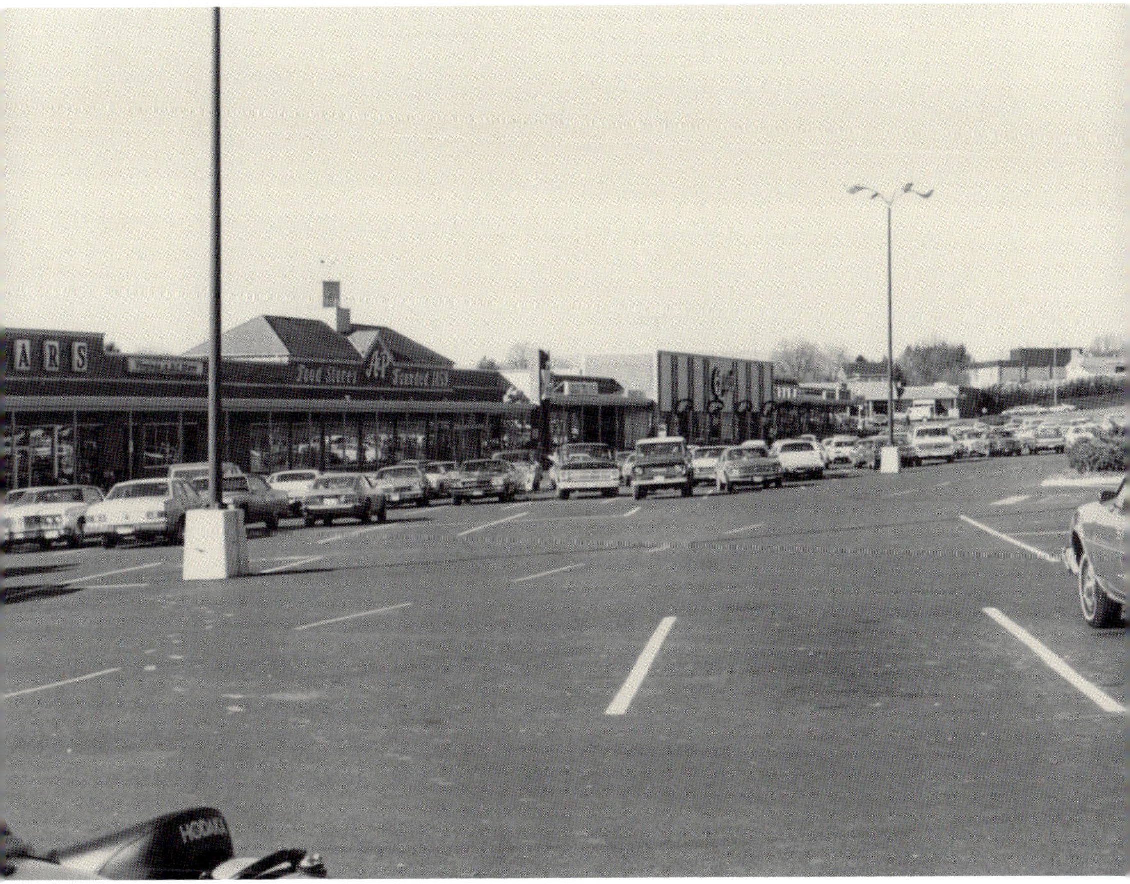

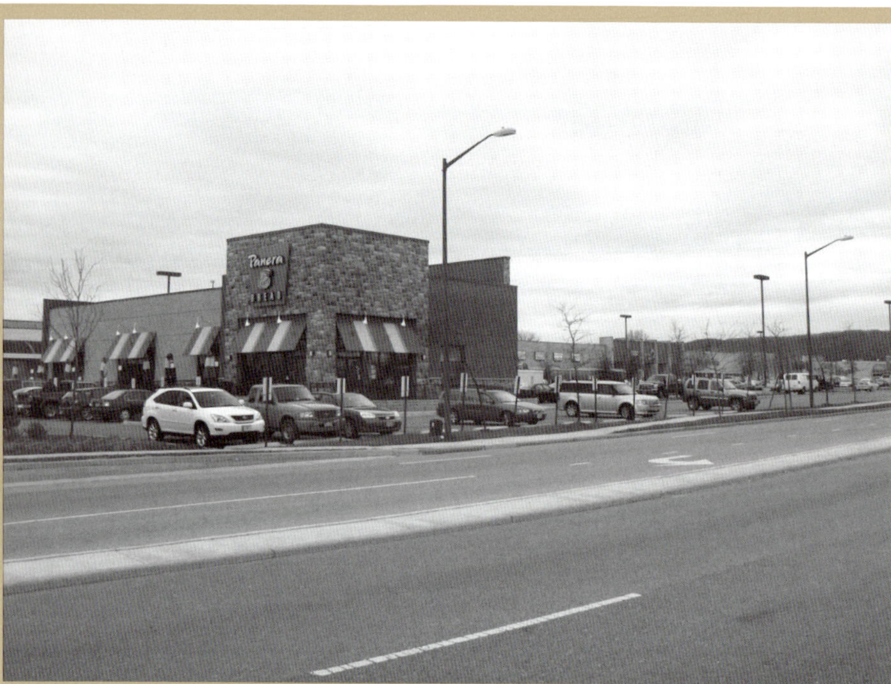

University Mall opened on University City Boulevard off Prices Fork Road in 1974. While some of the stores open to the outside, it is a small indoor mall with many businesses accessible only from the interior. Woolco was an anchor store here in 1976. The mall was recently renovated, providing additional parking to accommodate students at the Math Emporium, offices such as Rackspace, and businesses like the university's Volume 2 Bookstore. (DLA.)

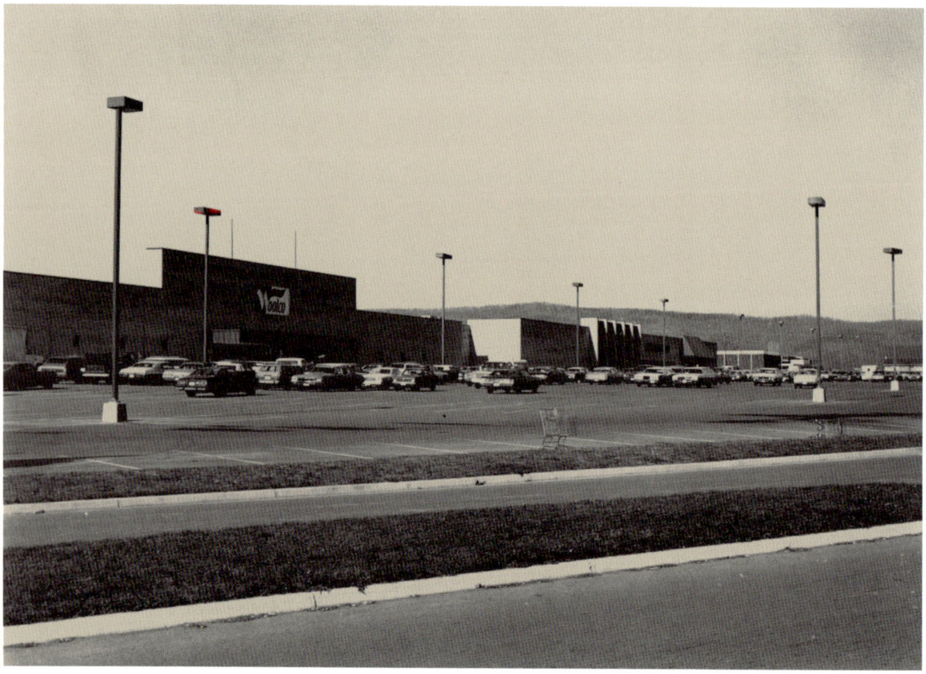

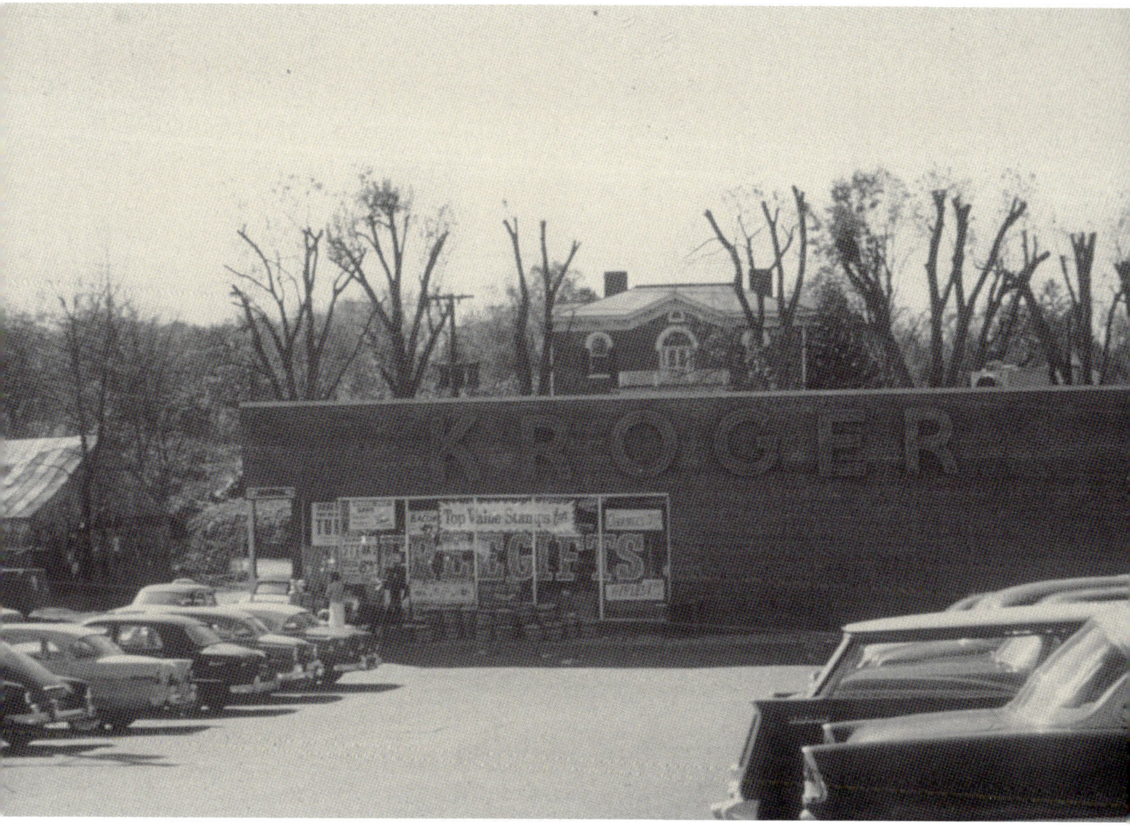

This Kroger supermarket was located on Main Street just south of the Roanoke Street intersection, across Draper Road from the Thomas-Conner House. Today, the building is home to the newly renovated Tech Bookstore. The facade is higher now, but one can just see the roofline of the Thomas-Conner House above the glass section of the building. (TOB.)

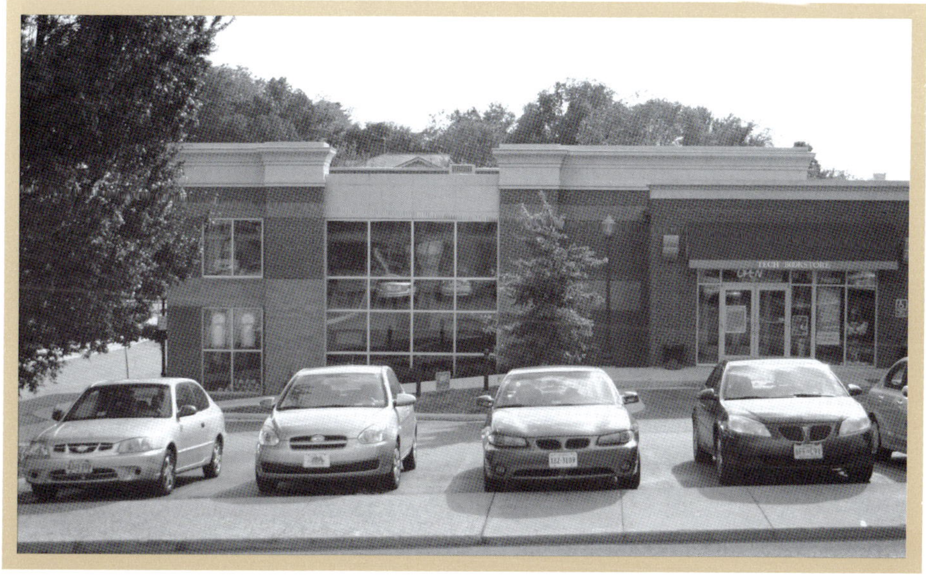

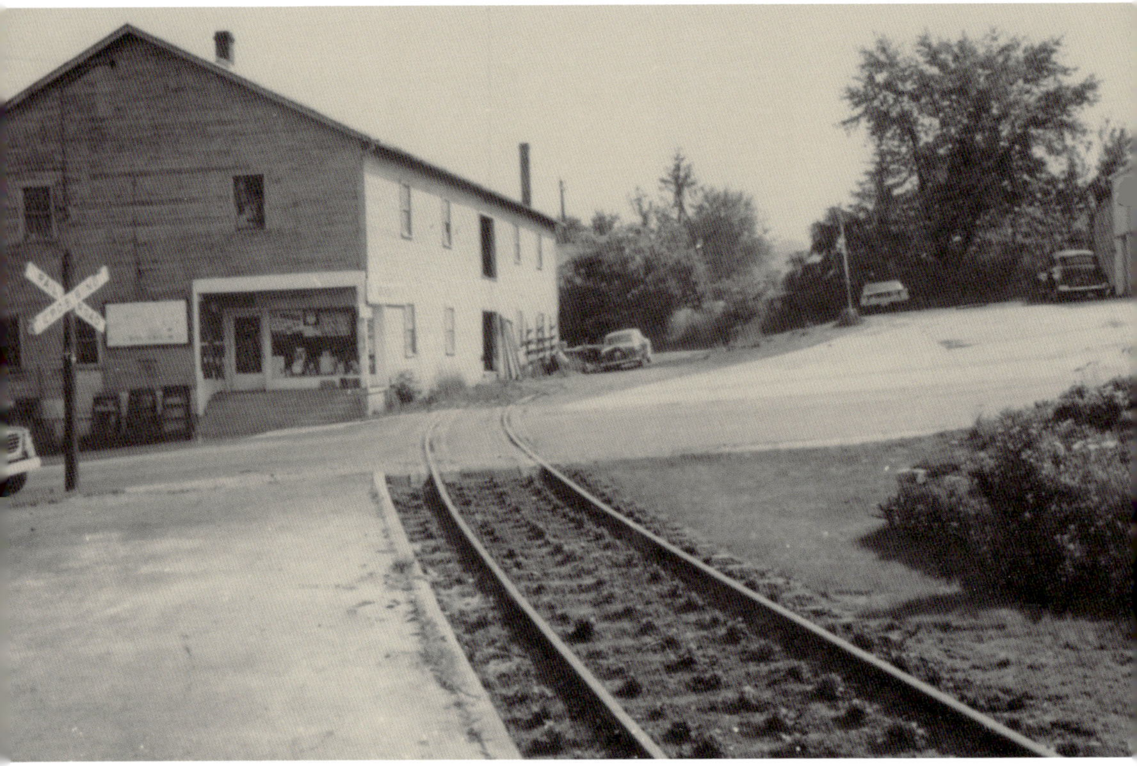

The Huckleberry Railway crossed Main Street from the depot—today's Blacksburg Municipal Building—to just south of the old Annie Kay's store at the corner of Washington Street. This spur served the Feed and Seed store located there. Better roads and more reliable automobiles led to the railroad's demise, and Virginia Tech, the largest freight user, preferred to invest in air transportation, requiring the removal of the railroad tracks to extend the airport runway. (JK.)

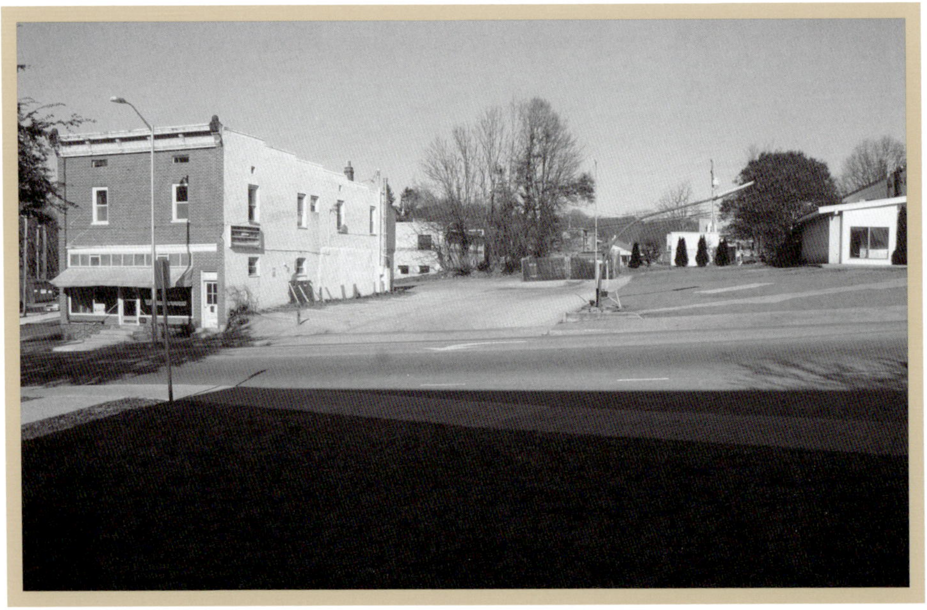

CHAPTER 5

RESIDENCES

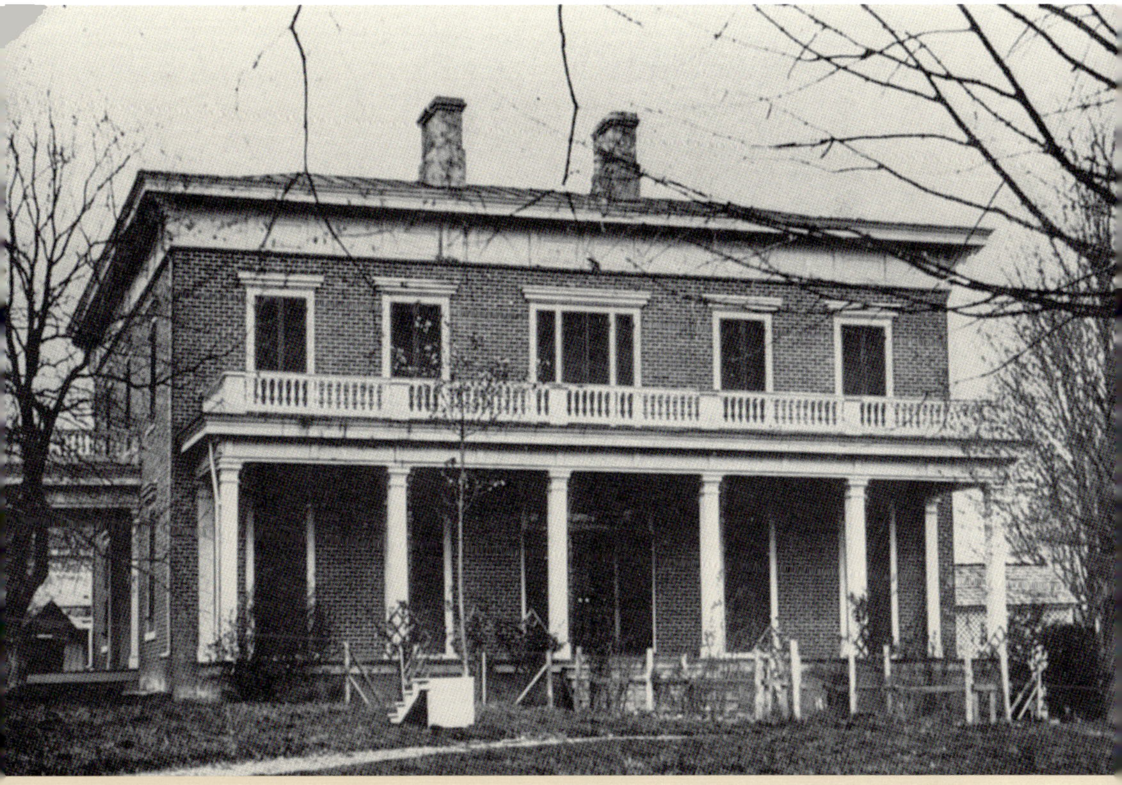

Blacksburg's residences reflect the town's progression from frontier edge to university town. Whitethorne, today located within the Hethwood development, was originally part of Smithfield Plantation. The house was built around 1850 for James Francis Preston, grandson of Smithfield's builder, Col. William Preston. The house has been in the Heth family since 1888. (DLA.)

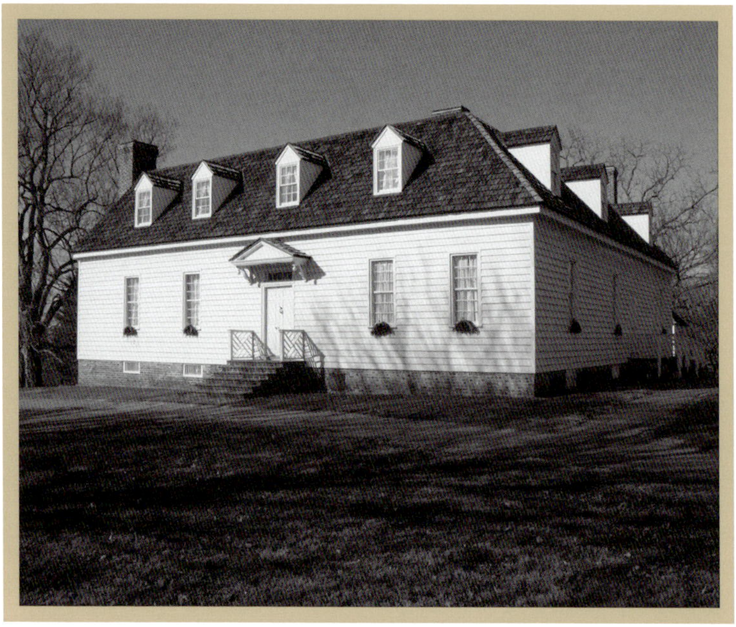

William Preston deliberately placed his 1774 house on a rise, providing panoramic views and summer breezes. It was built in an L shape, a funnel to channel the breezes through the windows on both sides of each room. The two porches were later additions and were removed during the 1960s restoration by Preservation Virginia. Note the fence near the home. Prior to restoration, Virginia Tech used the structure as a barn for hay storage. (SMFD.)

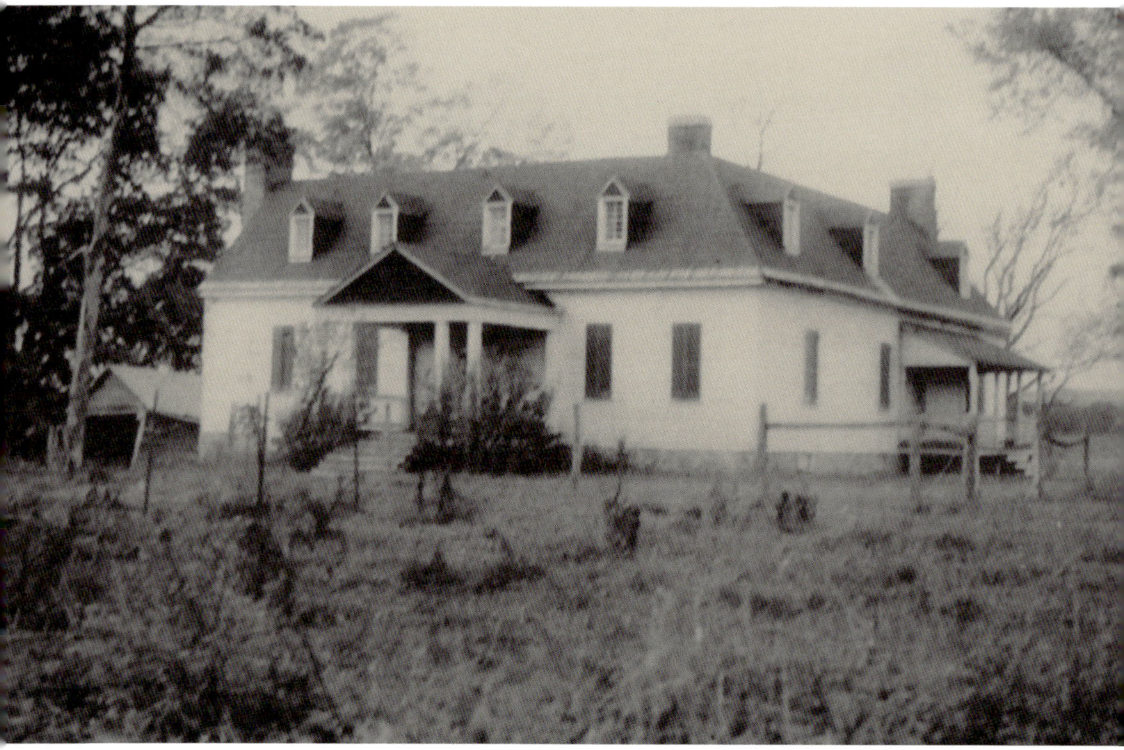

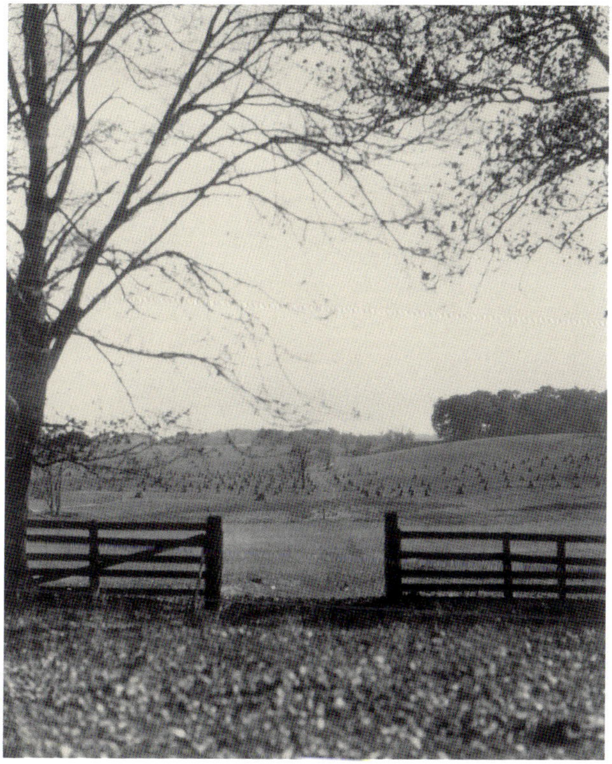

From the front gate of William Preston's Smithfield Plantation, there are remnants of a long, straight approach to the 1774 manor house, typical of wealthy plantation owners in colonial times. The hill on the right was the site of the overseer's cabin, and the Preston family cemetery is on another hill just out of sight on the left. In the modern photograph, Southgate Road bisects the old road. (SMFD.)

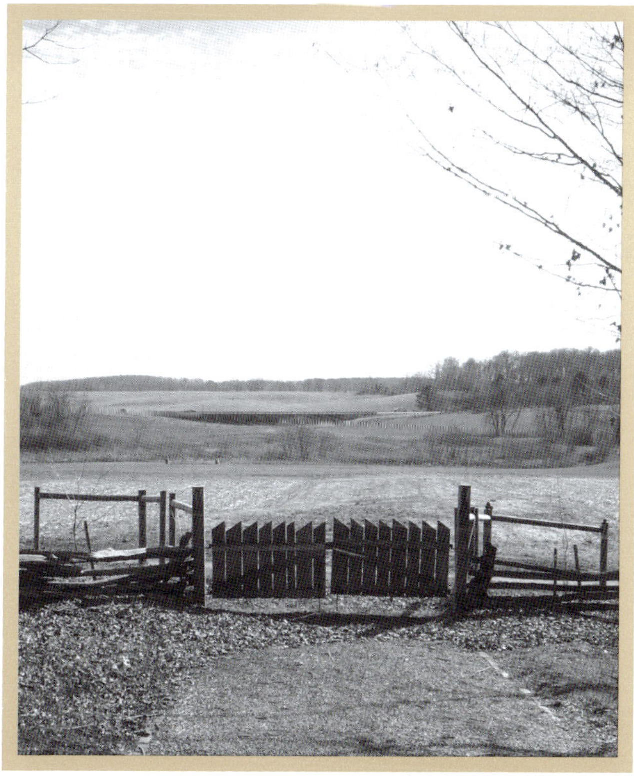

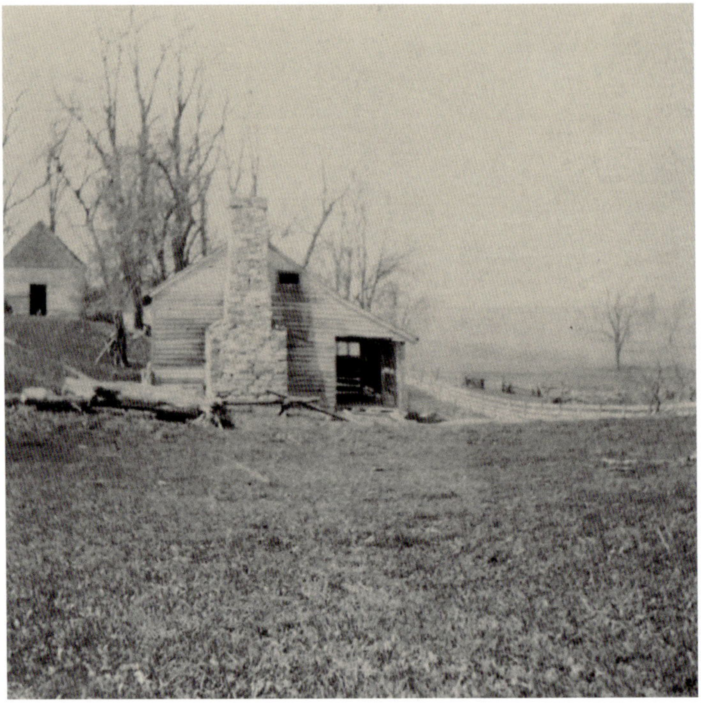

This photograph was used as evidence to reconstruct the cook's cabin and the smokehouse at Smithfield Plantation. The logs used to reconstruct the cabin came from another cabin at Whitethorne, on part of the plantation in what is now Hethwood. The cabin was where the slave cook lived. She had to cook in her own cabin during the summer to keep the heat of the fires out of the manor house. The Prestons held up to 90 slaves at Smithfield. (SMFD.)

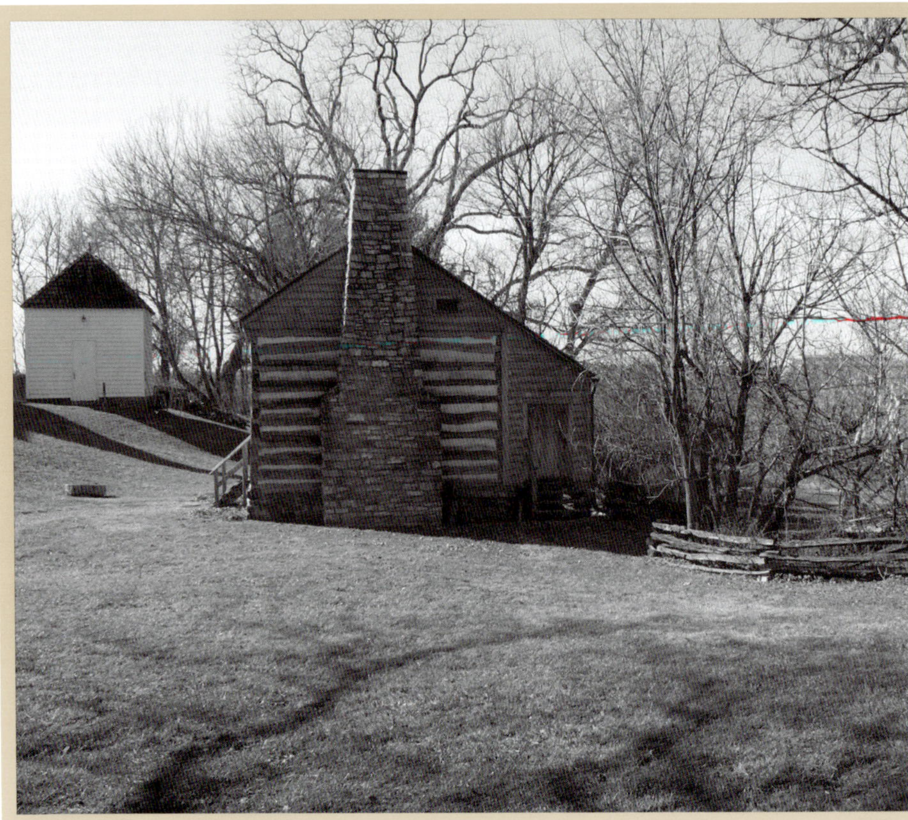

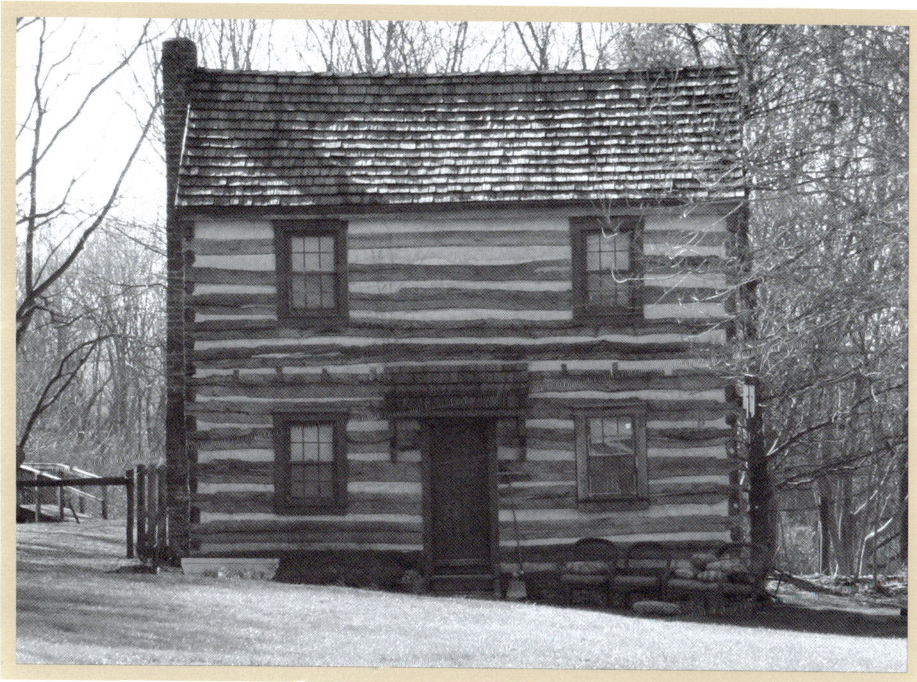

The ruin of a gristmill on the Smithfield property sits directly behind this cabin. James Patton Preston, second generation of the Preston family and governor of Virginia from 1816 to 1819, had the mill constructed in the early 1800s to replace a mill his father had operated much farther away from the manor house. The new mill was powered by damming nearby Strouble's Creek. The cabin was restored by Preservation Virginia in the 1980s and is currently known as the Miller's Cabin and rented as a residence. (SMFD.)

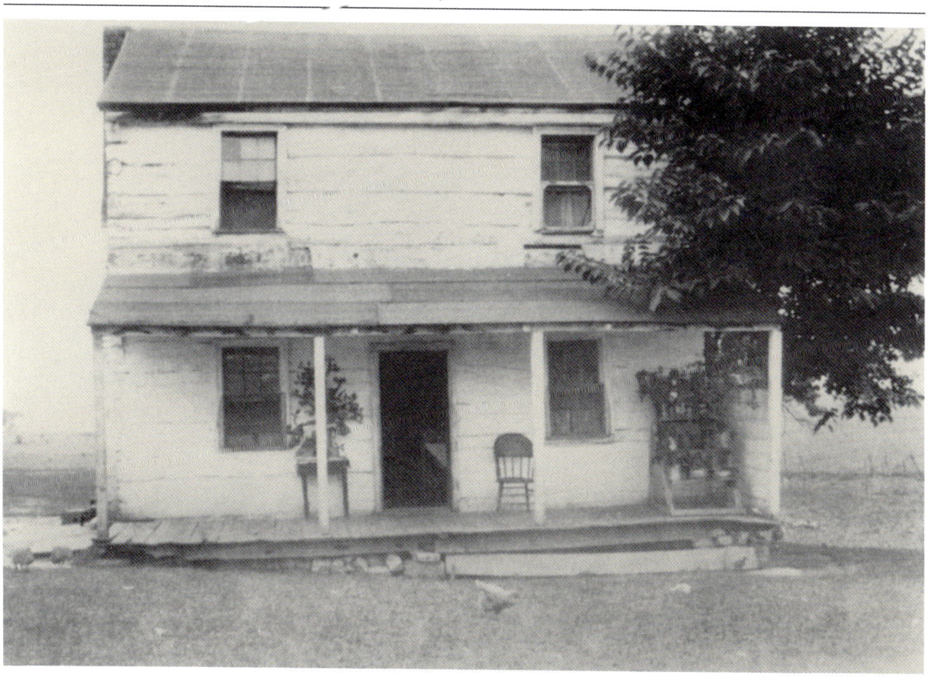

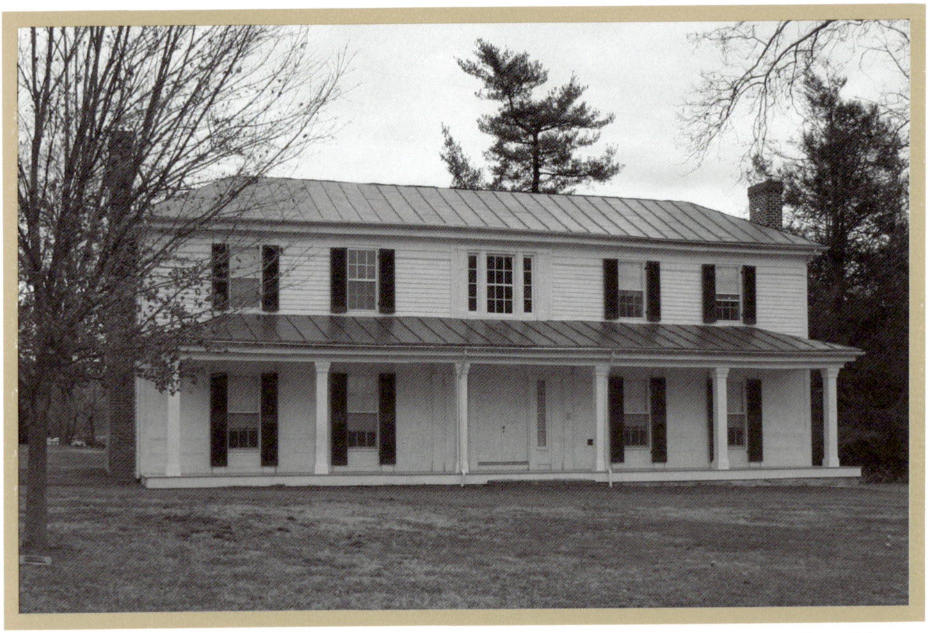

The oldest building on campus, Solitude was originally part of Smithfield Plantation. The first generation of Prestons built a log structure on the property, and the third generation constructed two significant additions, incorporating the original cabin into this Greek Revival–style home. Virginia Agricultural and Mechanical College—now Virginia Tech—acquired the property in the 1870s and completed a major restoration of the property in 2011. (DLA.)

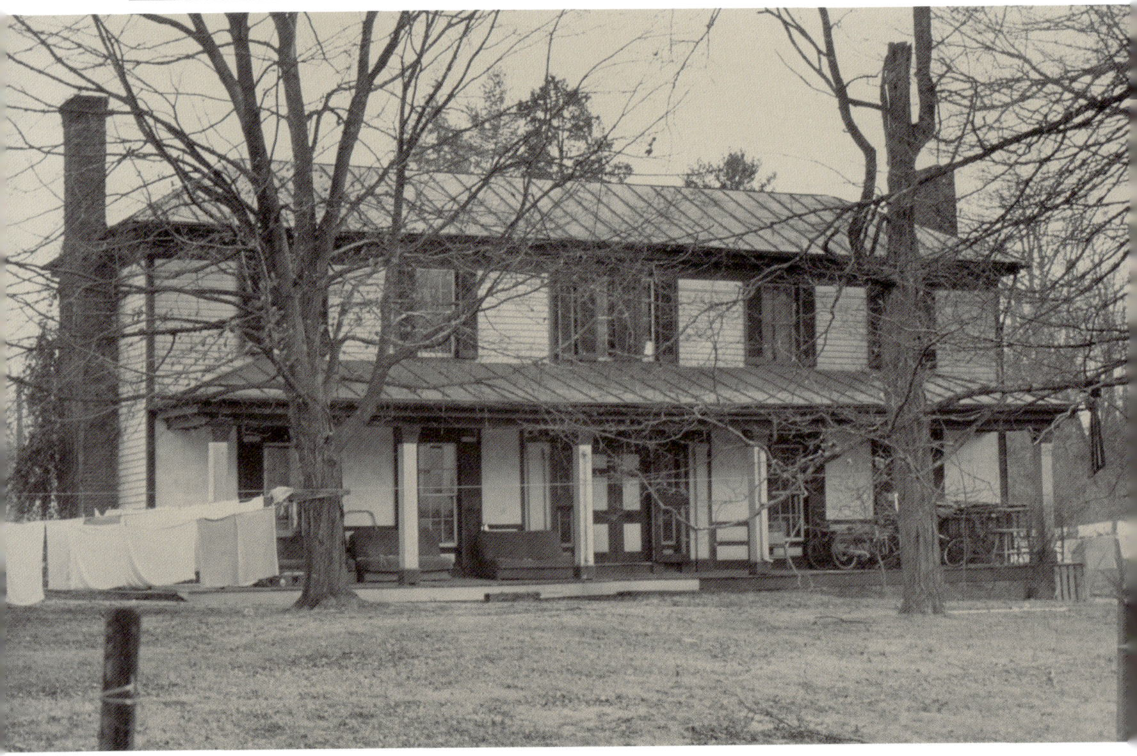

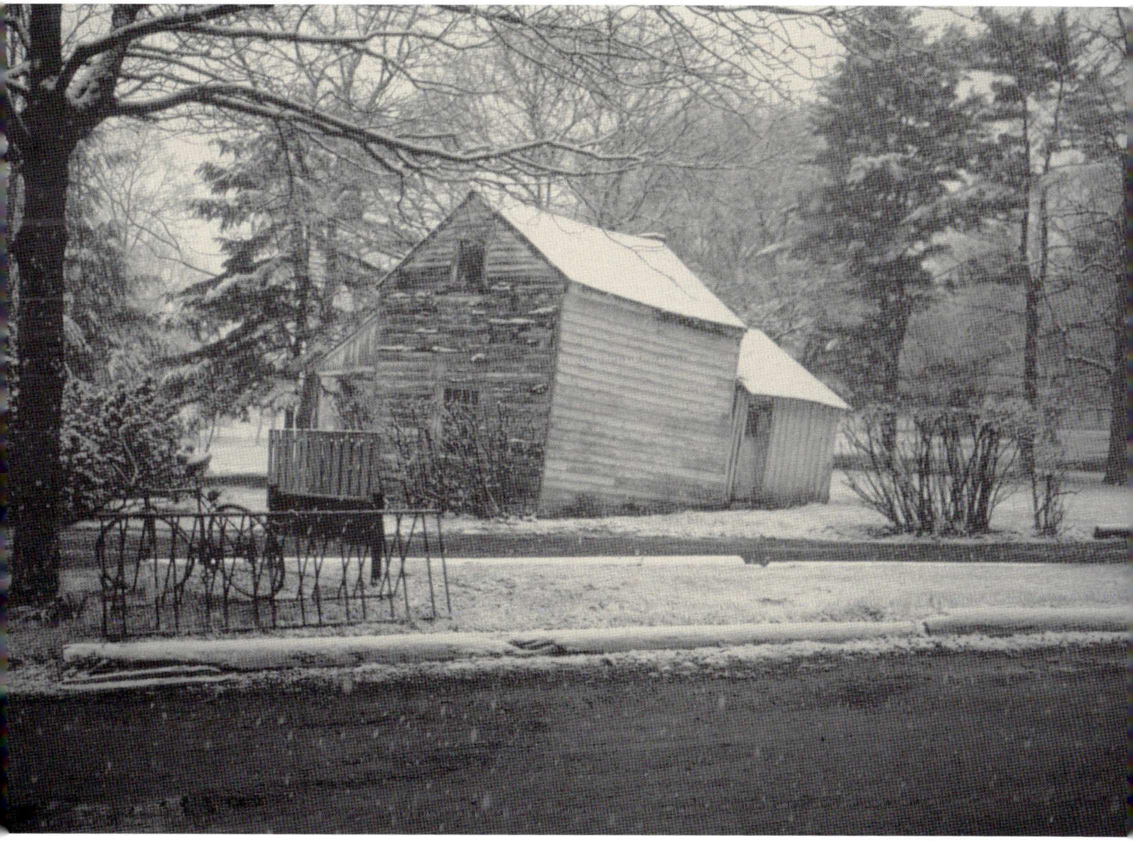

This log cabin was a slave house at Solitude during Robert Taylor Preston's antebellum residency at Solitude. The structure is characteristically simple: one main room downstairs with a side addition and a small attic loft. Notice that the cabin has clapboard siding, which was likely added very soon after construction, if it is not original. The cabin was fully restored by Virginia Tech after years of neglect from various uses. (SMFD.)

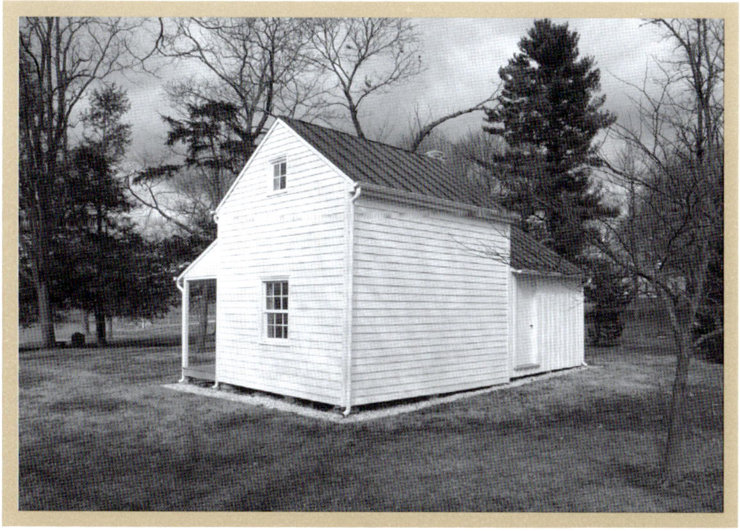

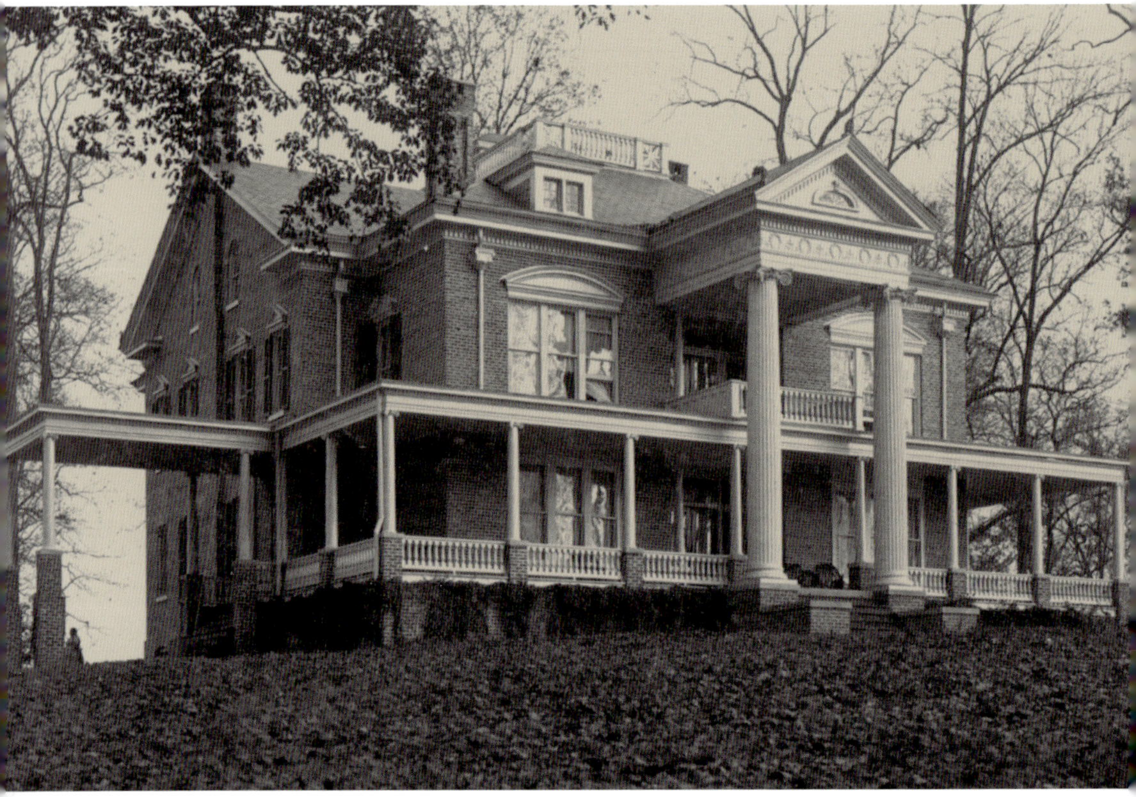

The Grove, located above the Duck Pond on the Virginia Tech campus, is the President's House. The home was built in 1902 for Virginia Tech president John M. McBryde. The house was inhabited by six presidents through 1971, when it became academic offices. After renovations in 1988, it was again used as the President's House. The Grove looks very much the same today as it did in the 1906 photograph above. (DLA.)

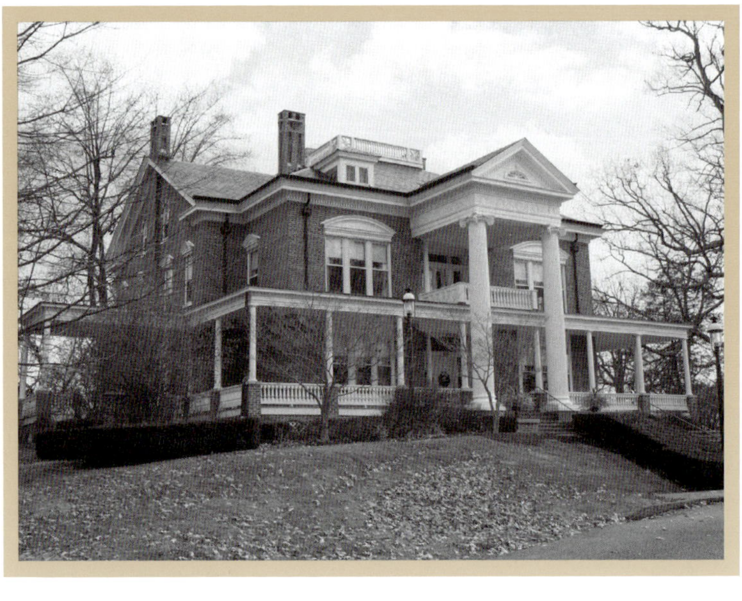

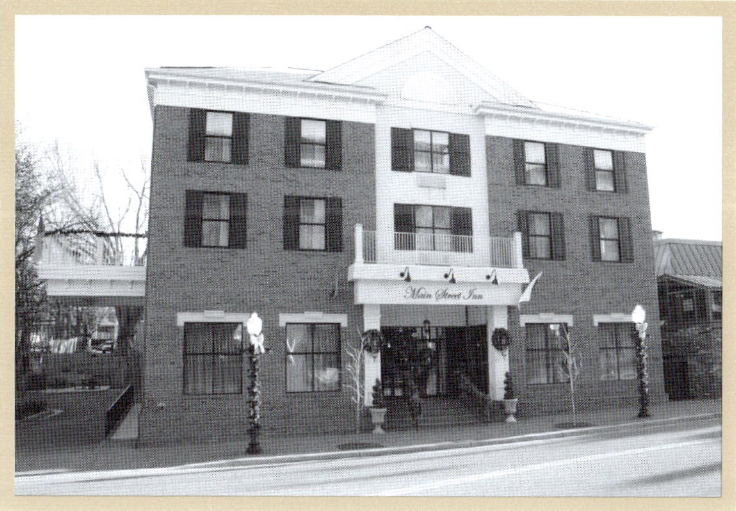

Main Street has changed dramatically over the years due to fire, community growth, and expansion of commercial uses into former residential spaces. Over the last decade, this growth has been particularly apparent with the development of the Main Street Inn and mixed-use buildings like Kent Square and Clay Court. Despite the changes, Main Street still retains a small-town feel. (DLA.)

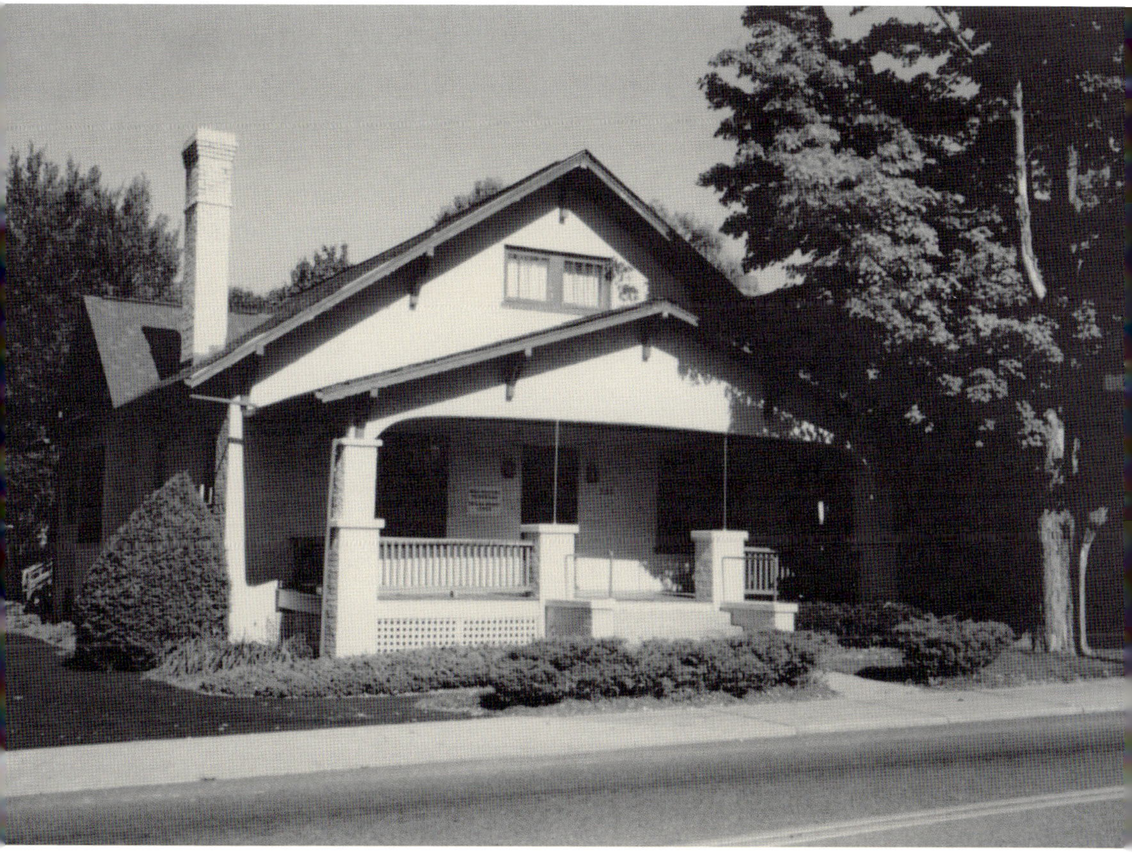

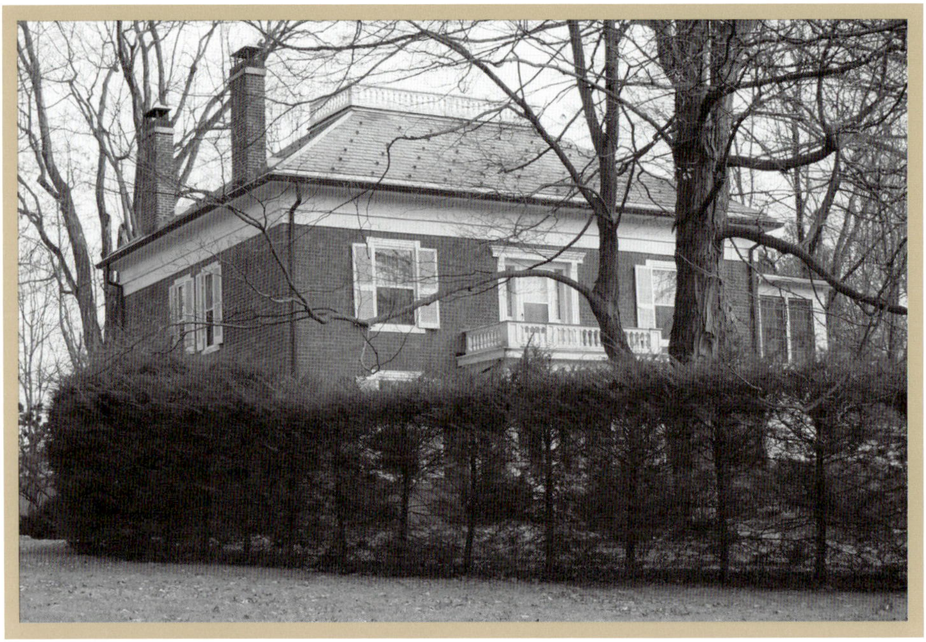

The Amiss-Palmer House was built in 1856 by Edwin Amiss, who had large landholdings along South Main Street. The house, today located at the end of Mountain View Drive, once had a commanding view of the road to the front and mountains to the rear. The house and 450 acres of surrounding land were purchased by Col. W.H. Palmer in 1880. The land was subdivided in the 1950s, leaving three acres around the house. (DLA.)

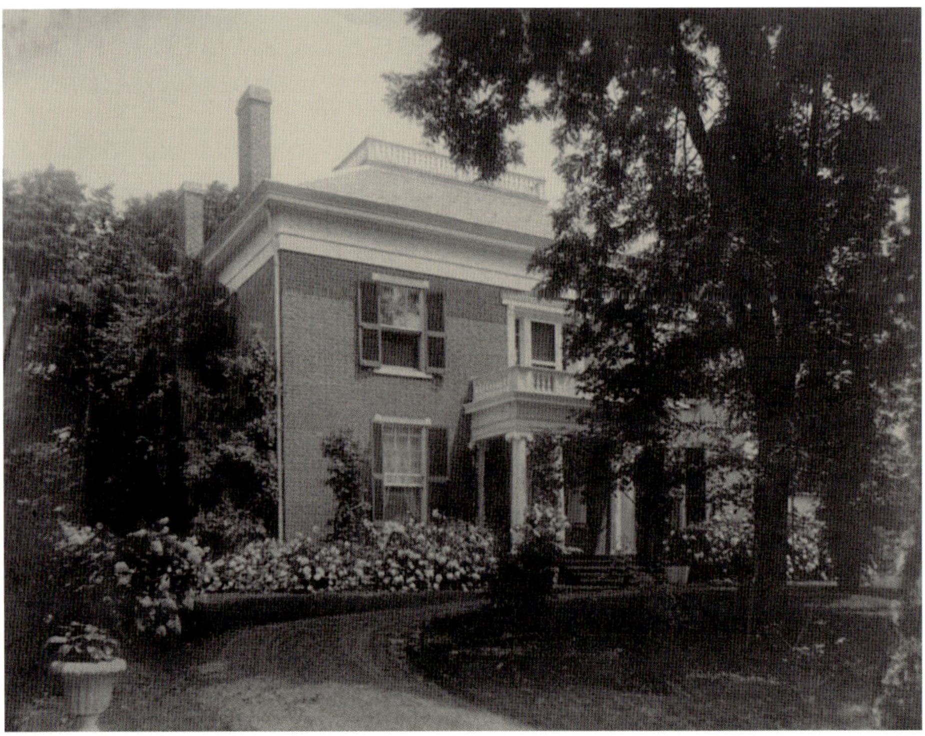

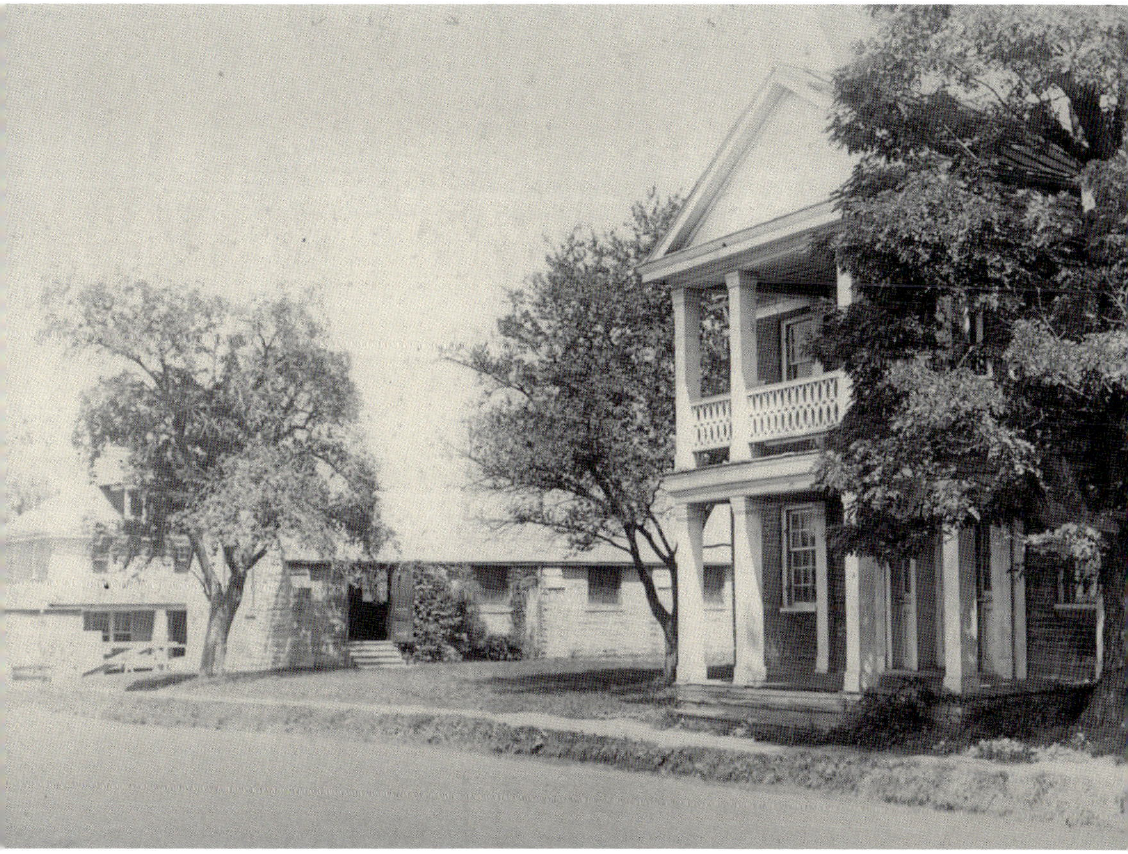

In the early 1800s, William Lybrook owned the entire block around Christ Episcopal Church. This home stood next to the 1874 sanctuary for the church and was torn down when the church tower was added in 1934. Lybrook is the namesake for Lybrook Row, which was to the right of this home. Nearly all of Lybrook's property has been acquired from his heirs by the church, including the Canterbury House located behind the church. (CEC.)

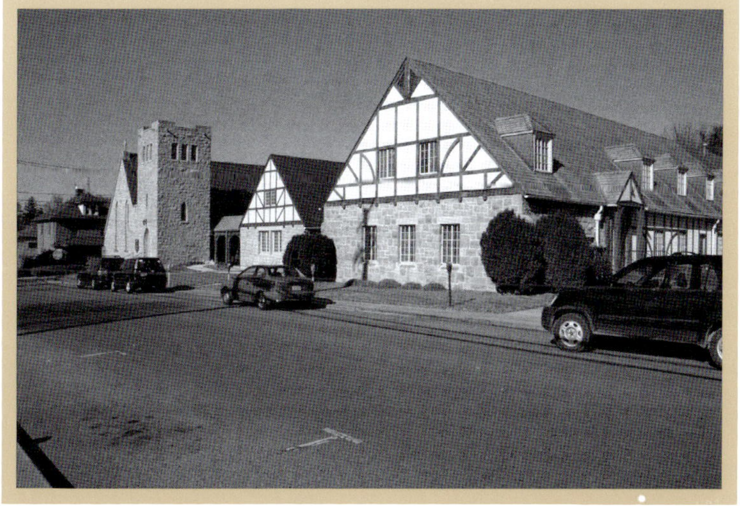

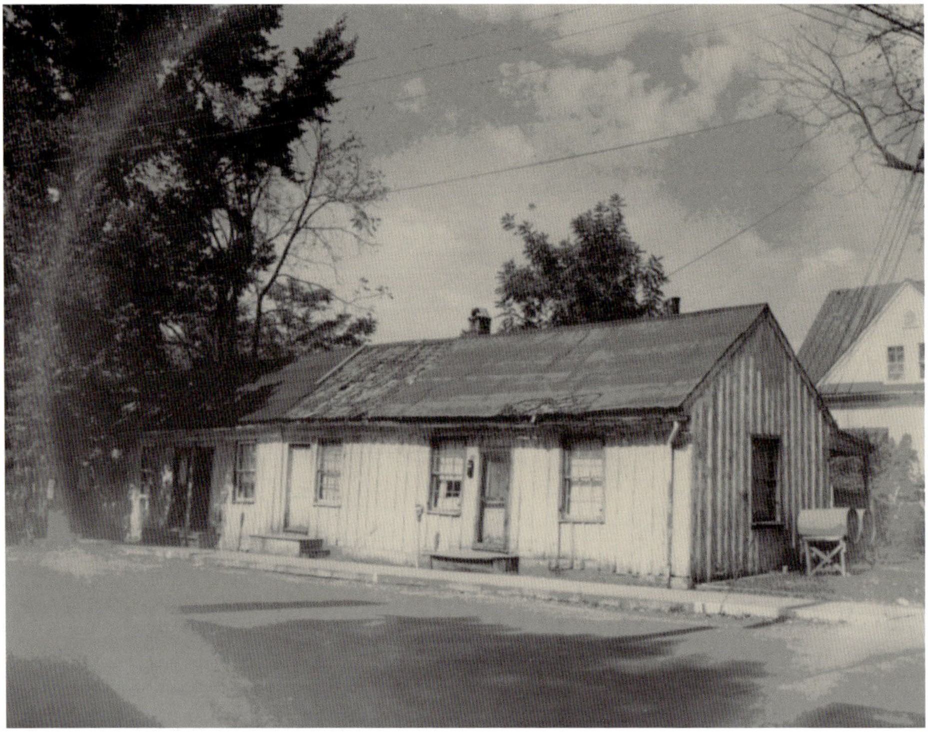

Lybrook Row was located at the corner of Roanoke and Church Streets, on land now used by Christ Episcopal Church for their preschool program. The building was clearly in a state of disrepair when the above photograph was taken prior to its demolition in the 1970s. Lybrook Row was used as housing for Virginia Tech cadets before Lane Hall was constructed and was known by many around town as Hell's Row or Buzzard's Roost. (CEC.)

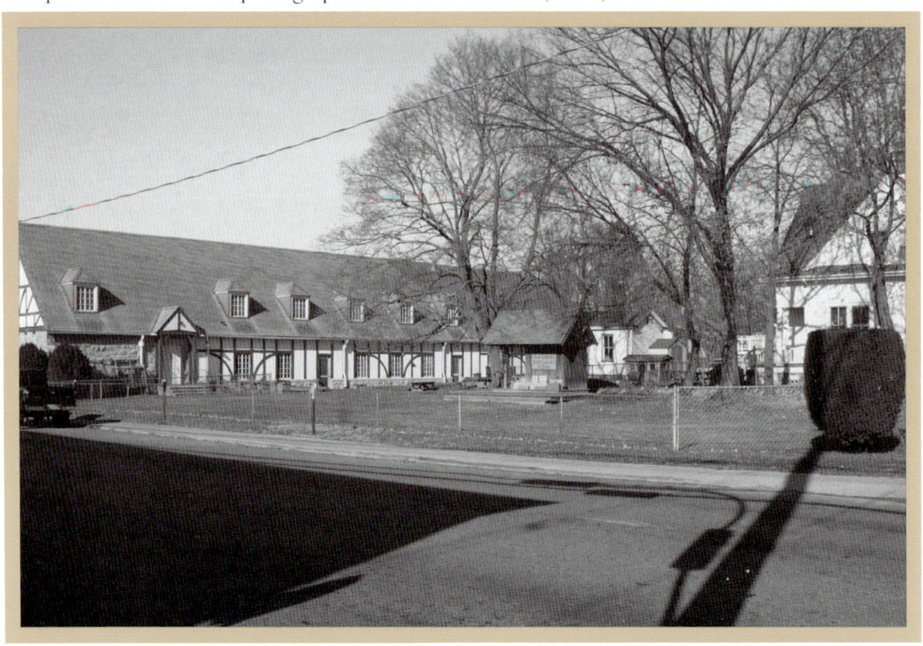

CHAPTER 6

TOWN AND CAMPUS MEET

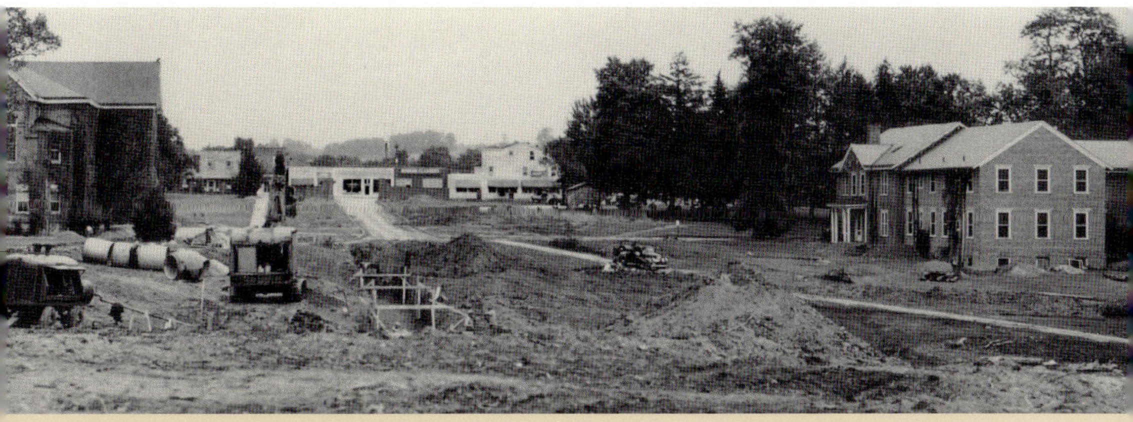

Construction of the Alumni Mall connecting the Drillfield to Main Street began in 1950 to accommodate future campus expansion. The project was controversial for its destruction of the woody grove between what is now Brodie and Rasche Halls and Henderson Hall and Squires Student Center. Today, the Alumni Mall is a major approach to campus. (DLA.)

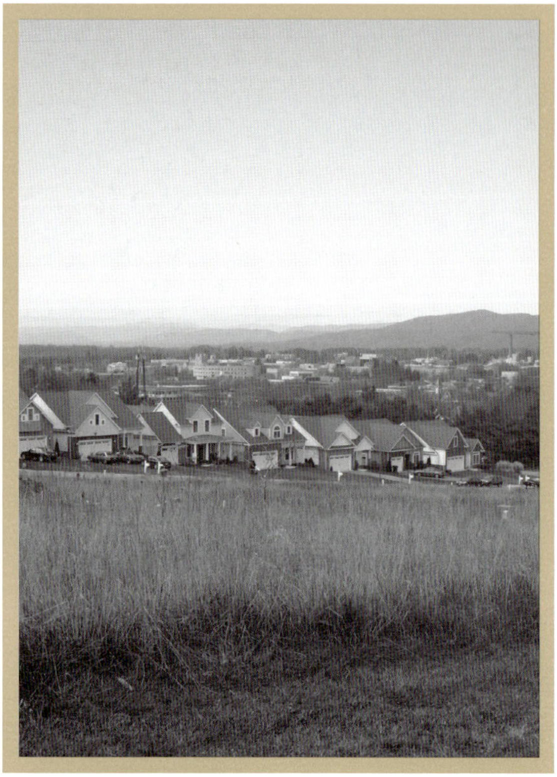

Blacksburg is surrounded by mountains and hillsides that provide beautiful views of the valleys below. These views of town from near the Municipal Golf Course show the growth of the town's original Sixteen Squares and the university's central campus since this 1879 photograph. (DLA.)

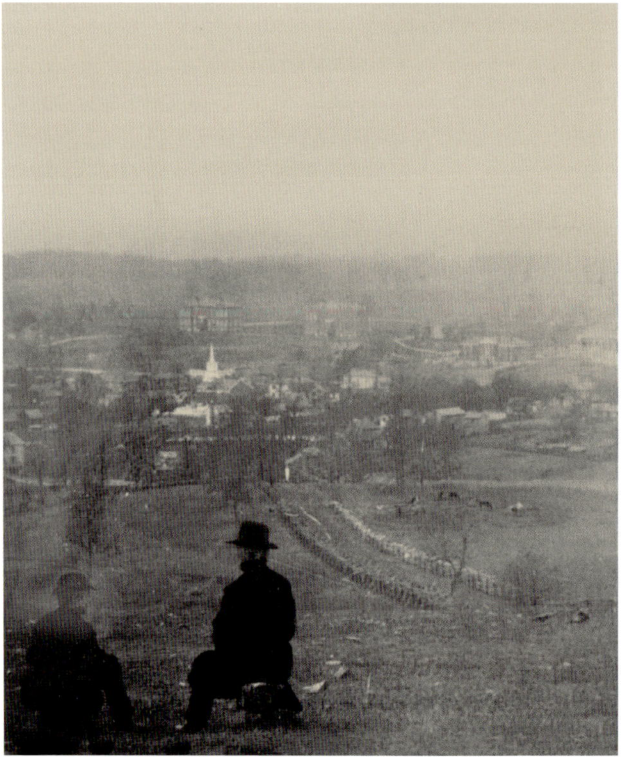

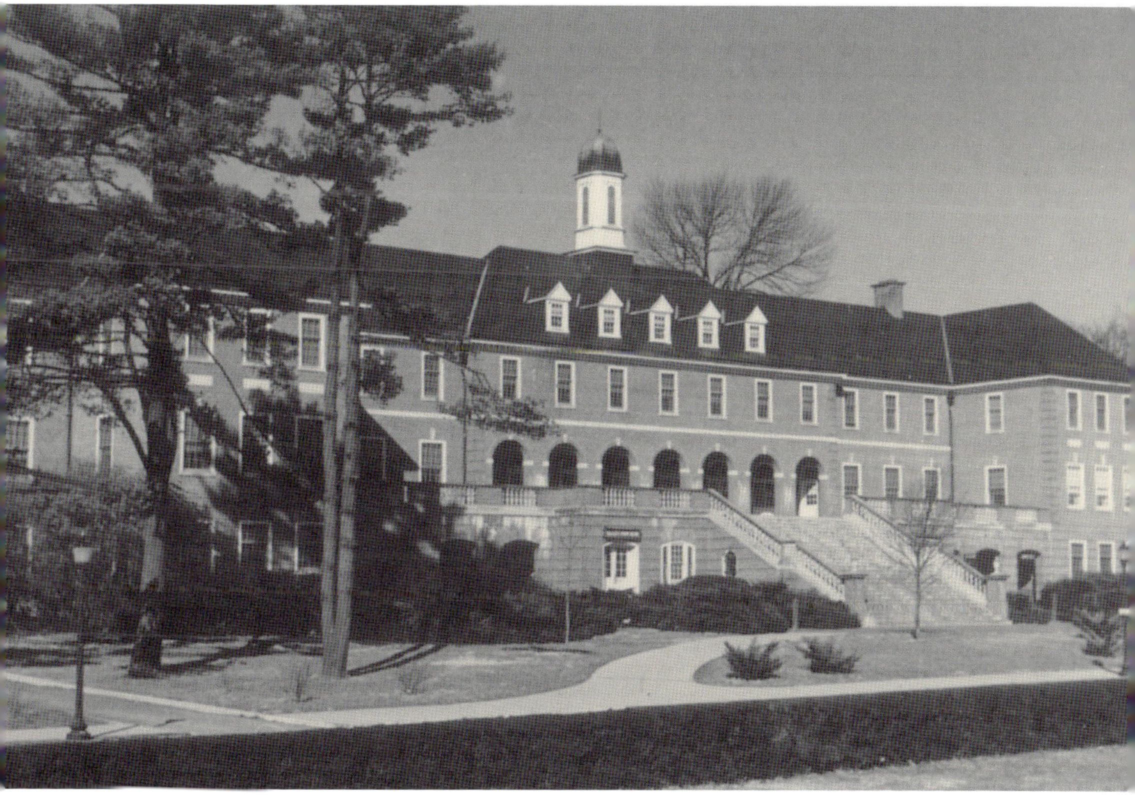

The original Squires Student Center was constructed in 1937 and named for an alumnus who made a large donation towards the building's completion. Additions completed in 1969 surround the original building, whose brick arches and dormers are visible from inside. Today, the building is a hub of activity for students and townspeople with ballrooms, theaters, an art gallery, a food court, and student activities offices. (DLA.)

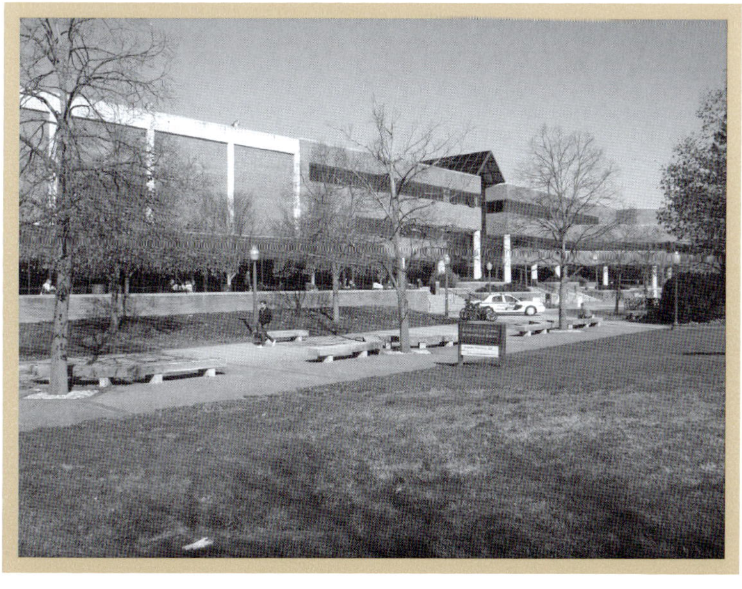

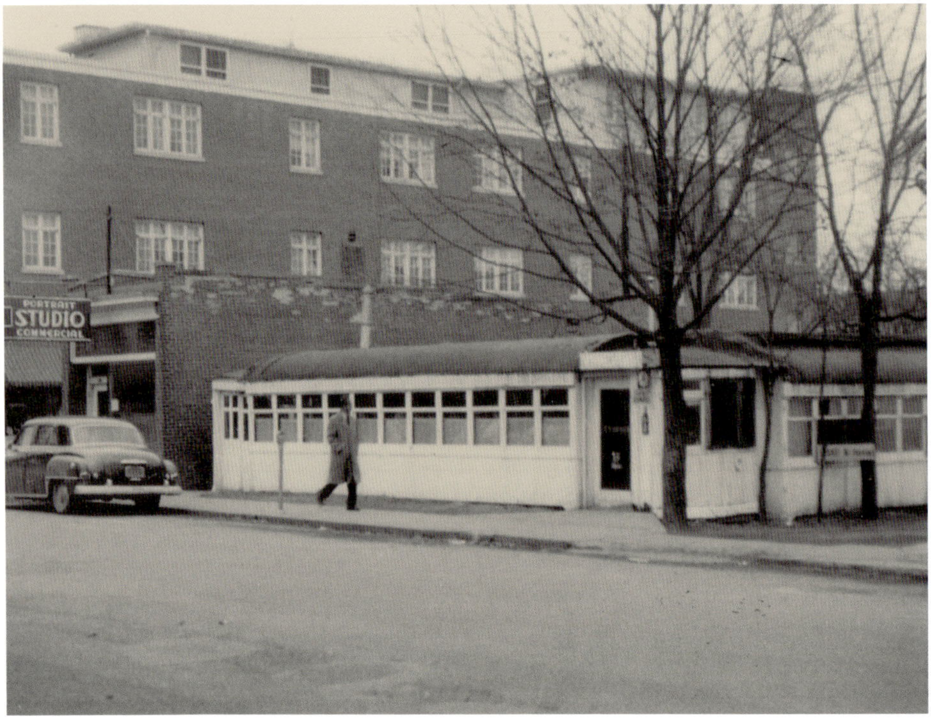

Meredith's was a classic 1950s diner, constructed from a railroad car with a lean-to built onto the back. Tech alumni recall that the food and service were excellent and that owner Ralph Meredith always knew his regulars. When it was razed for new construction on College Avenue, Meredith took over as manager of the dining hall on campus. The site has changed significantly but continues to house students' favorite restaurants. (JK.)

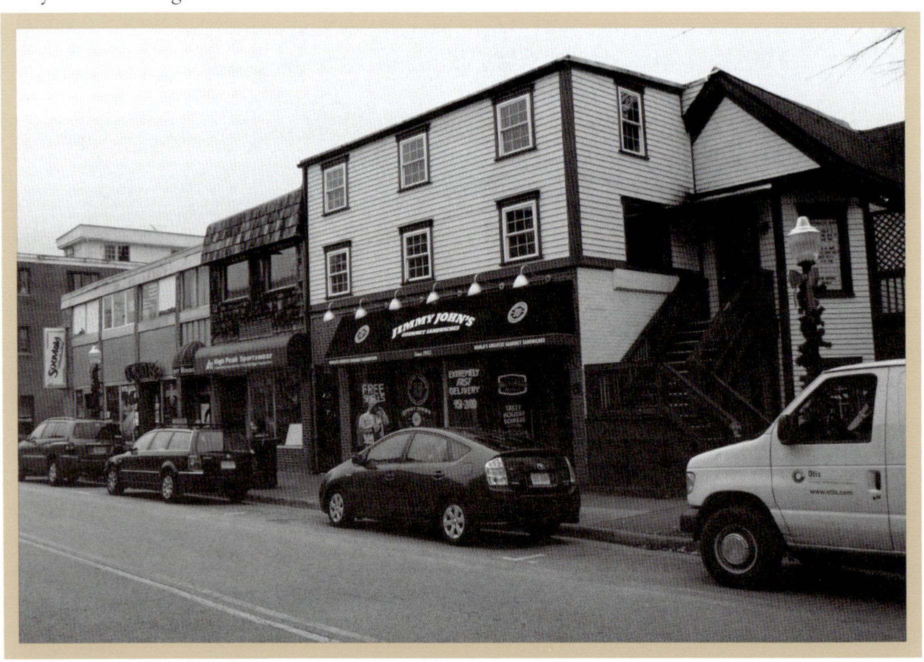

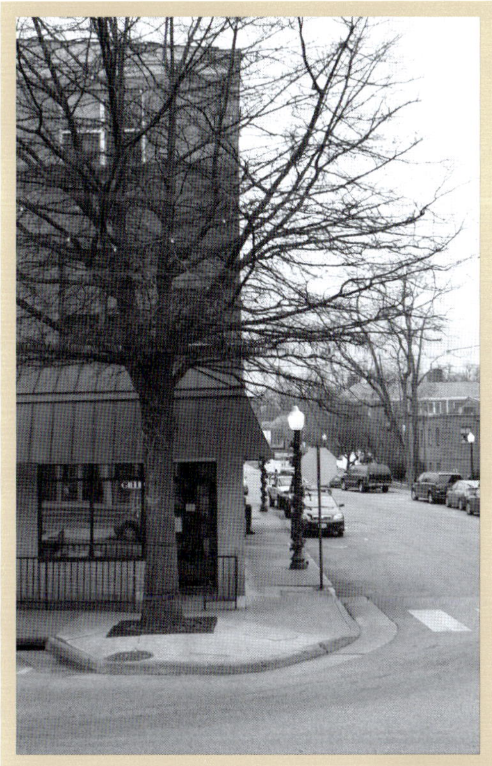

The 3.5-story Mill Building has been a large presence on the edge of campus for over 120 years. When operating as a water-driven lumber mill, it gave College Avenue an industrial feel that repelled other development. Eventually the location was too good to ignore and student-focused businesses swept in. Gillie's and the River Mill are popular restaurants housed within the large building, and there are apartments on the upper floors. Strouble's Creek still flows within the building's basement. (JK.)

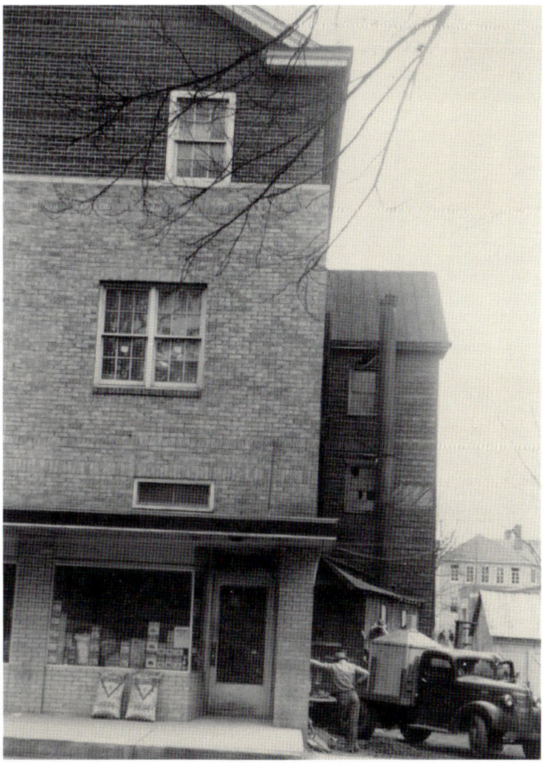

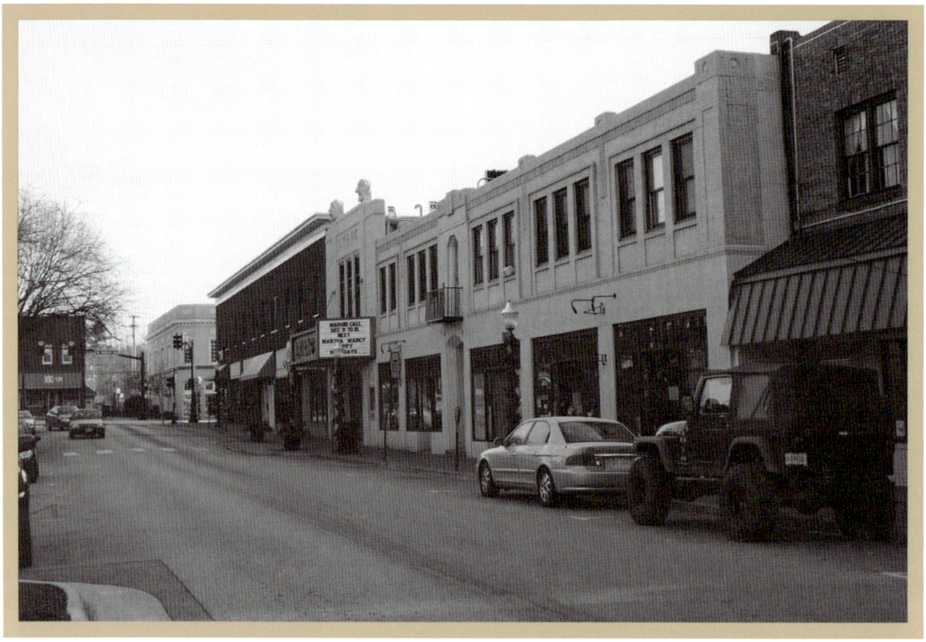

The Douglas Fairbanks Jr. film *Safari* was on the marquee at the Lyric Theatre in this 1940 view of College Avenue from campus. The entrance to the theater is on College Avenue, but the theater itself is parallel to the street, behind the building facades in the foreground of the photographs. The Corner Drugstore and Ellett Building are in the background. (DLA.)

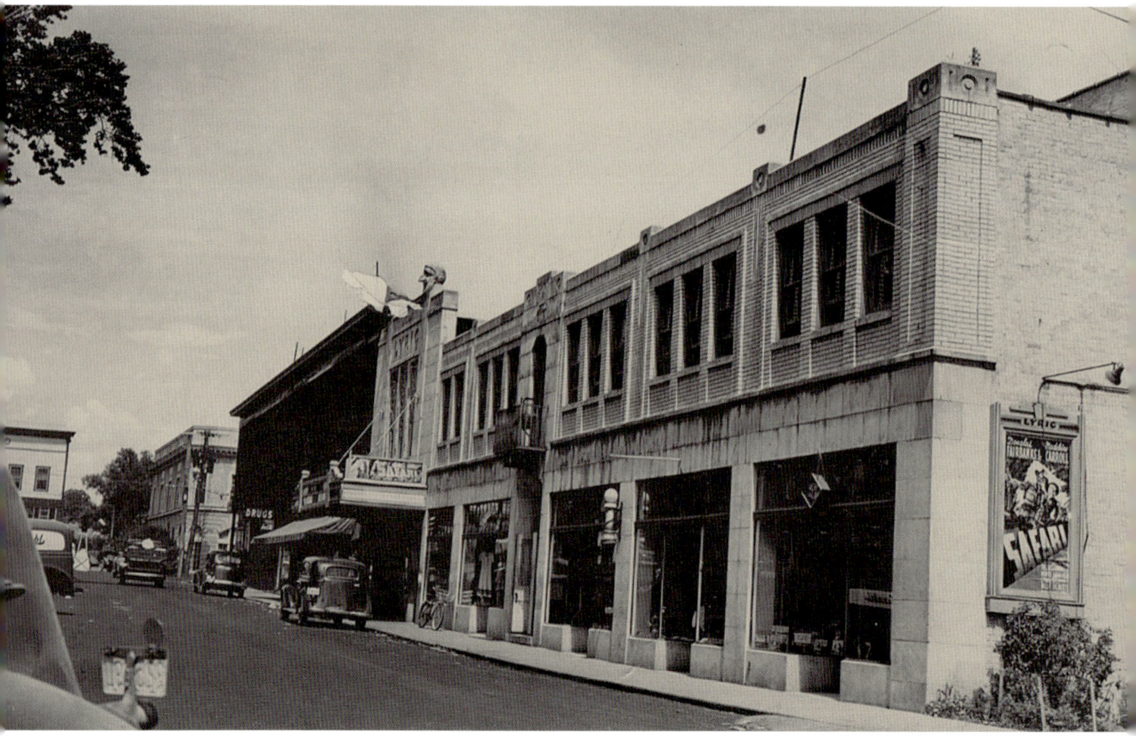

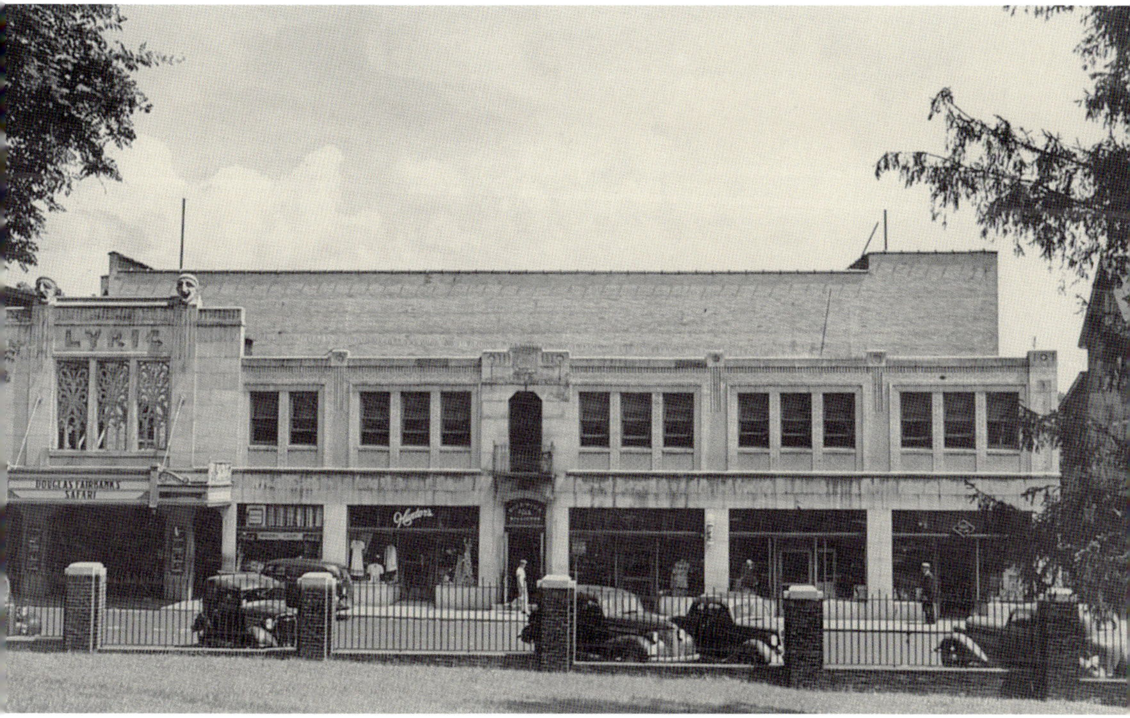

The Lyric Theatre opened in 1909 on North Main Street near the end of the Alumni Mall. In 1930, the theater was moved to College Avenue and was one of only three theaters in Virginia built for the new "talkies." After closing in 1989 and being used for classroom space, the Lyric was restored to its Art Deco and Spanish Colonial Revival glory in the 1990s. It reopened to the public in 1998 as a nonprofit movie and community theater. (DLA.)

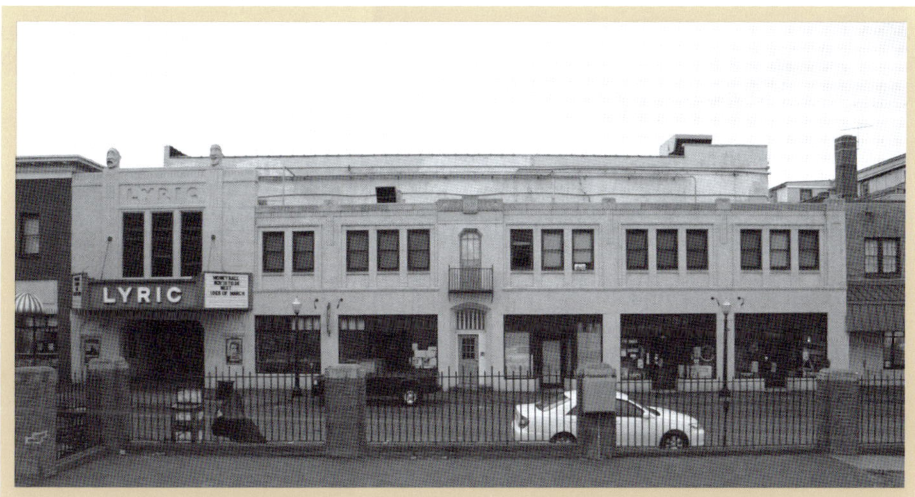

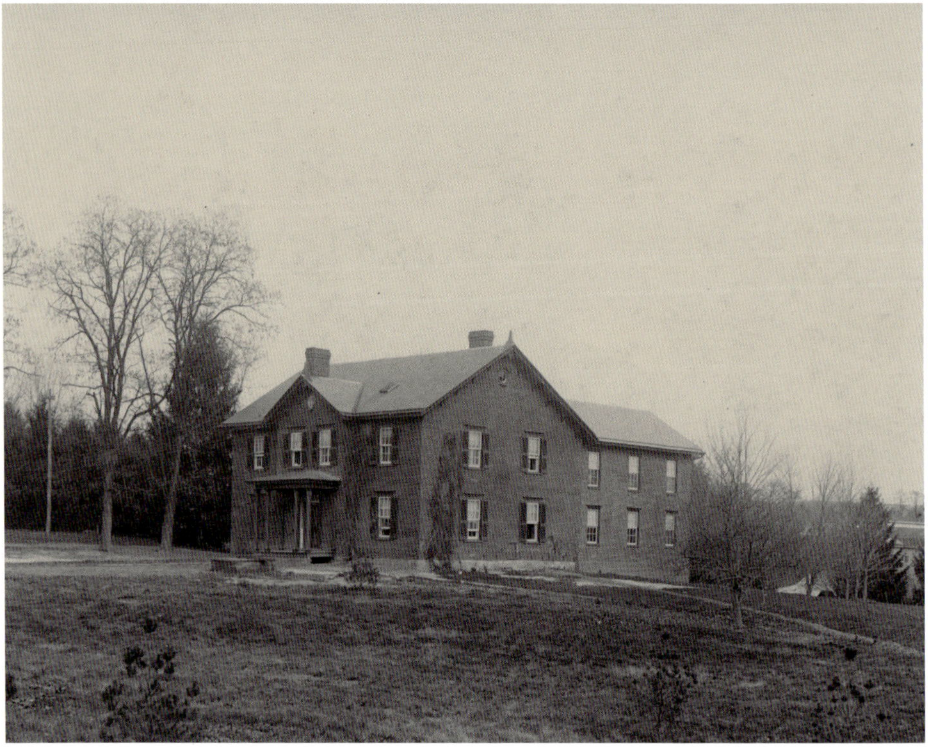

The oldest part of Henderson Hall, at left in the photograph below, was built in 1876 as the home of Virginia Tech's first president, Charles L.C. Minor. After the new president's house at the Grove was built in 1902, Henderson was expanded to become the infirmary. Henderson Hall, named for the college physician, Dr. William F. Henderson, became an academic building in 1998 when the infirmary was moved to McComas Hall. The building now houses music, theater, and arts programs. (DLA.)

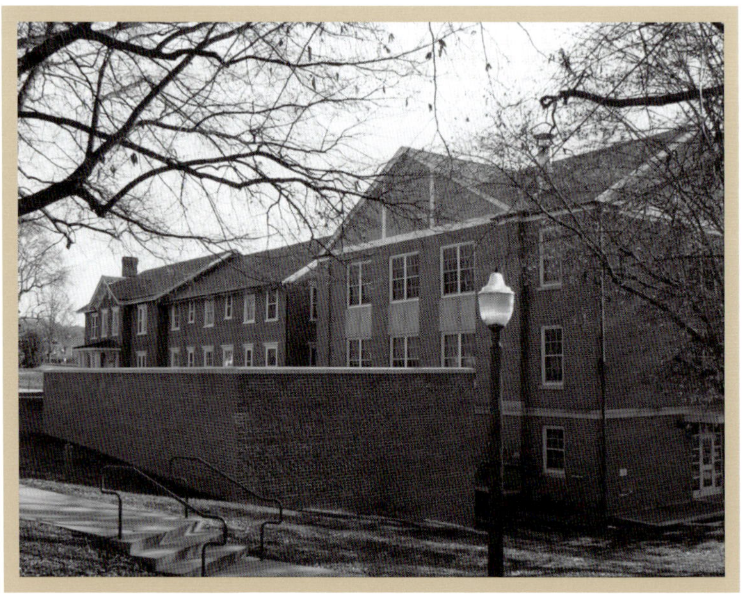

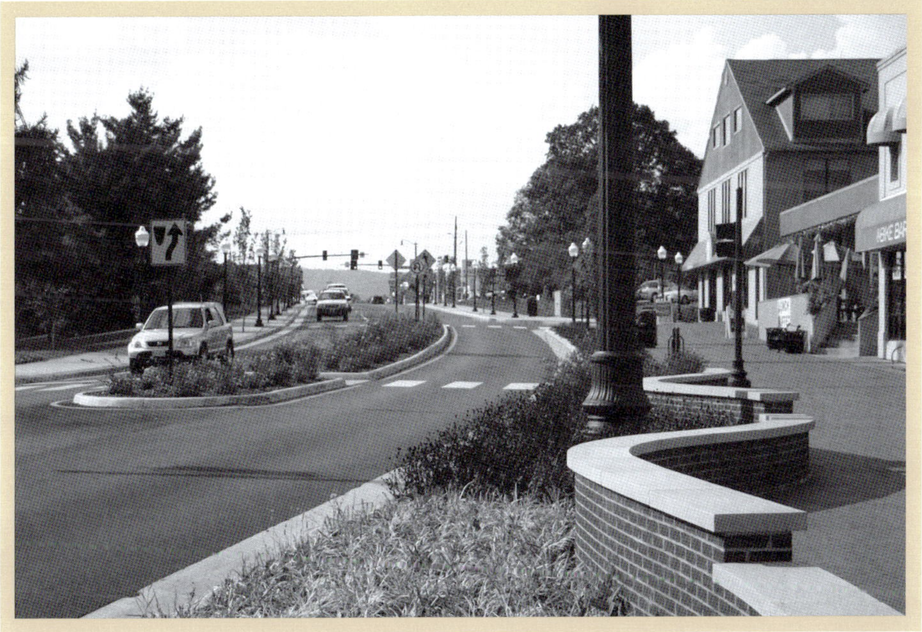

North Main Street was first widened in the 1930s to accommodate vehicular traffic generated by the university. Subsequent widenings created a mass of pavement dangerous for pedestrians to cross. Traffic-calming measures in 2011 resulted in narrower streets, a beautification of the approach to downtown, and a more pedestrian-friendly environment. (DLA.)

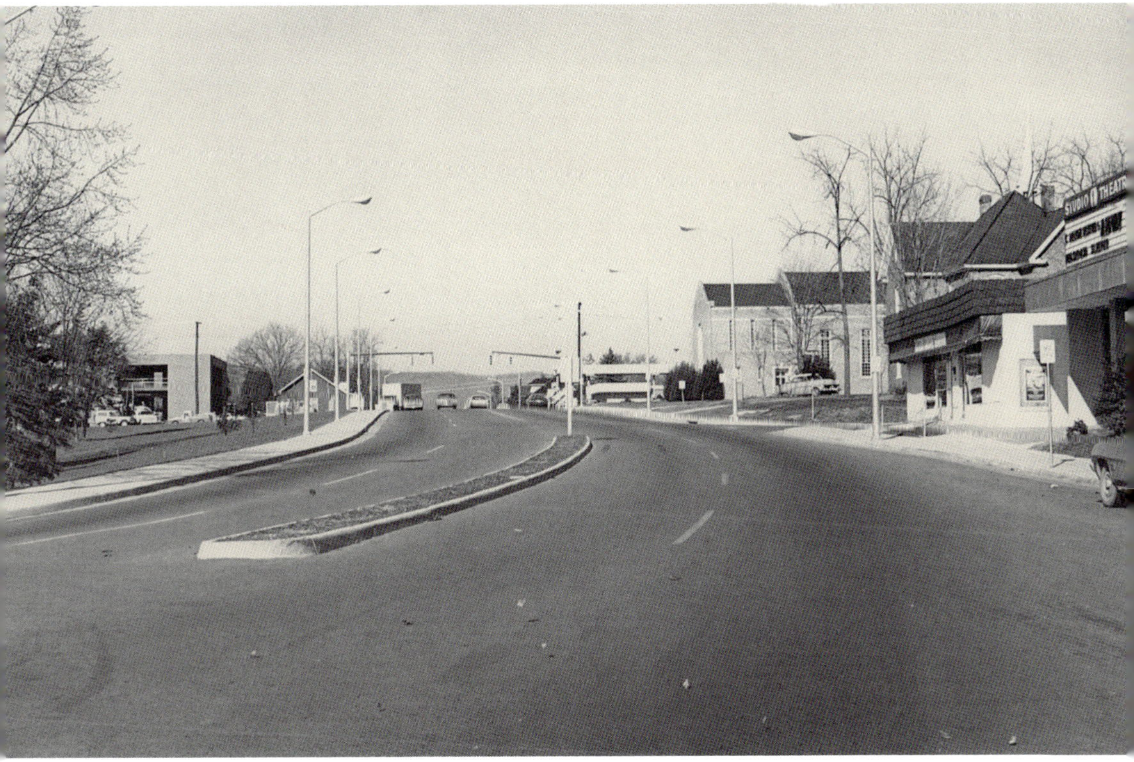

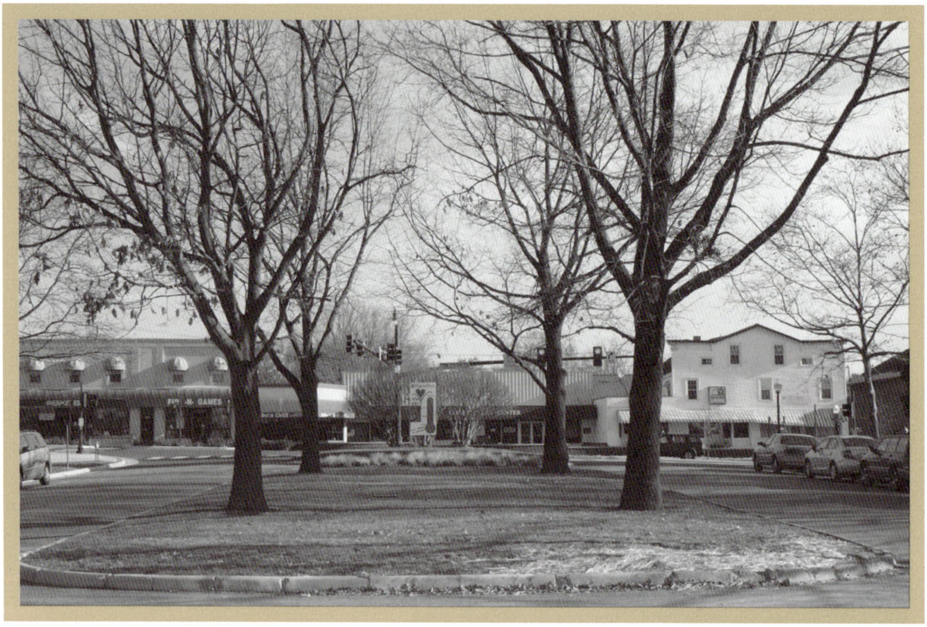

This 1950s view across North Main Street from the Alumni Mall shows structures in the Main Street "jog" constructed around the Preston and Olin Institute building. These businesses catered directly to students, such as the dry cleaners popular with Corps of Cadets members who needed their uniforms cleaned and pressed. (TOB.)

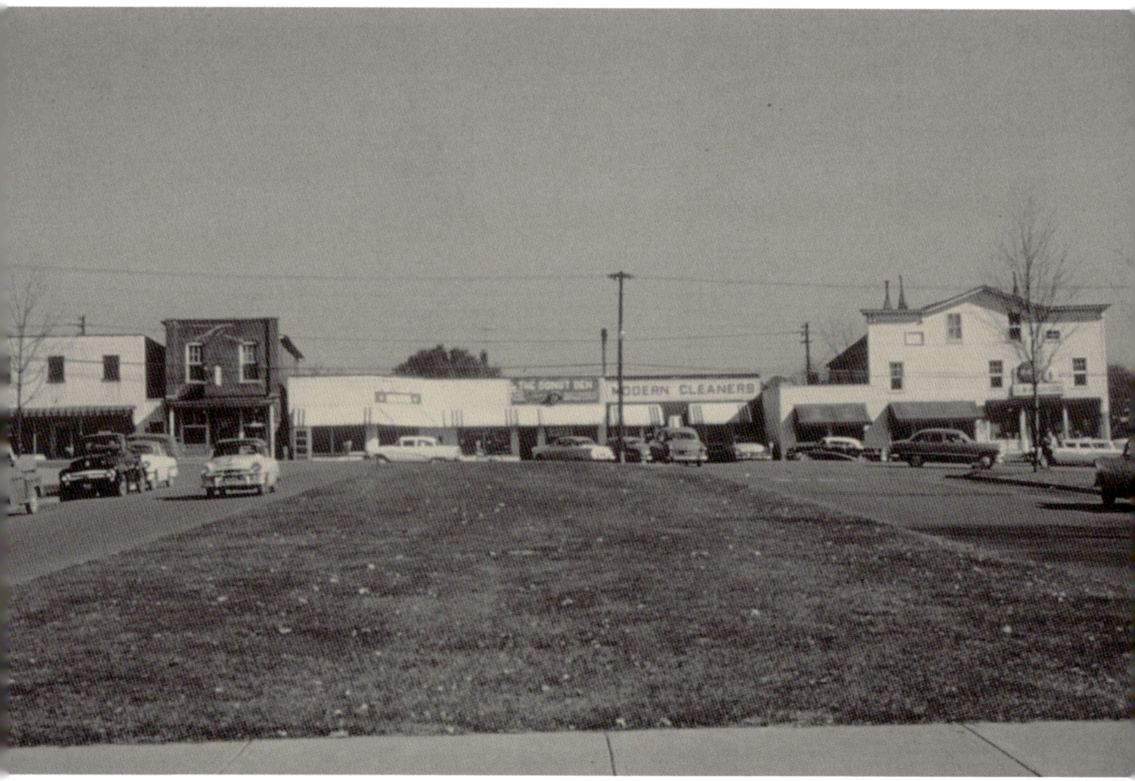

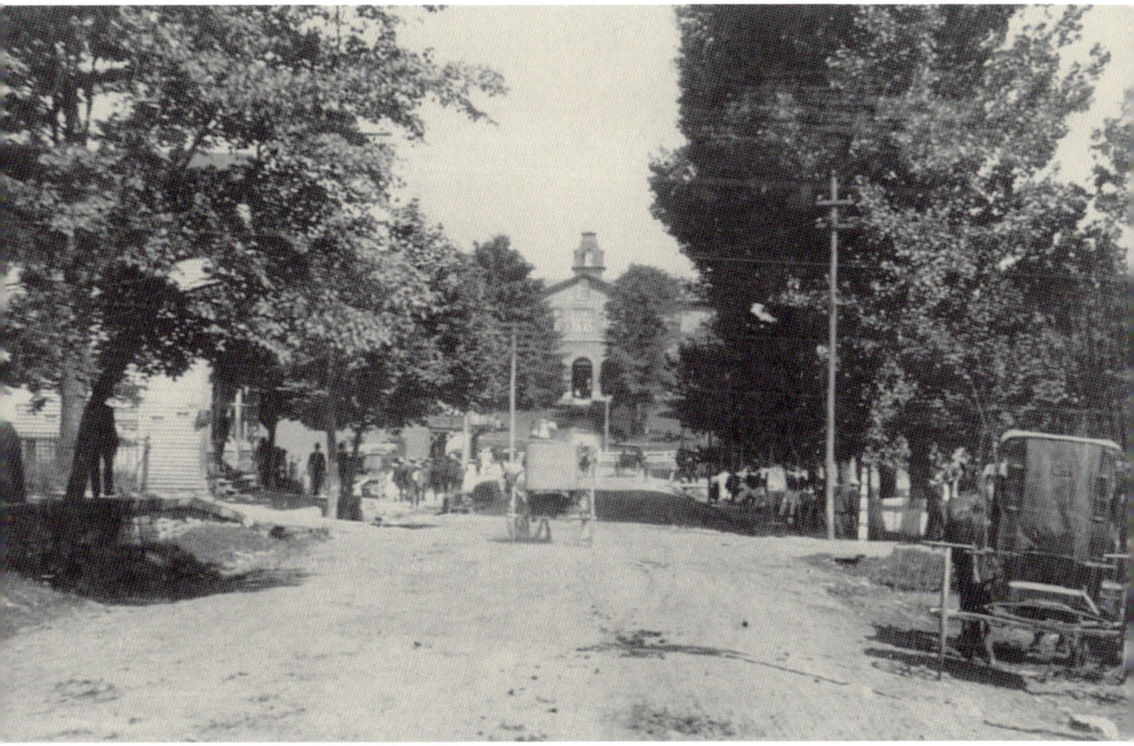

Buildings on Main Street jog to the right today as the road moves north from the College Avenue intersection. The reason for that jog is visible in this historical photograph from 1890. The Preston and Olin Institute building, later known as the Shops, was constructed at the end of Main Street in 1855. As the town grew around the campus, Main Street extended around the building. The Shops burned in 1913. Today, Main Street travels over the spot where the Shops once stood. (DLA.)

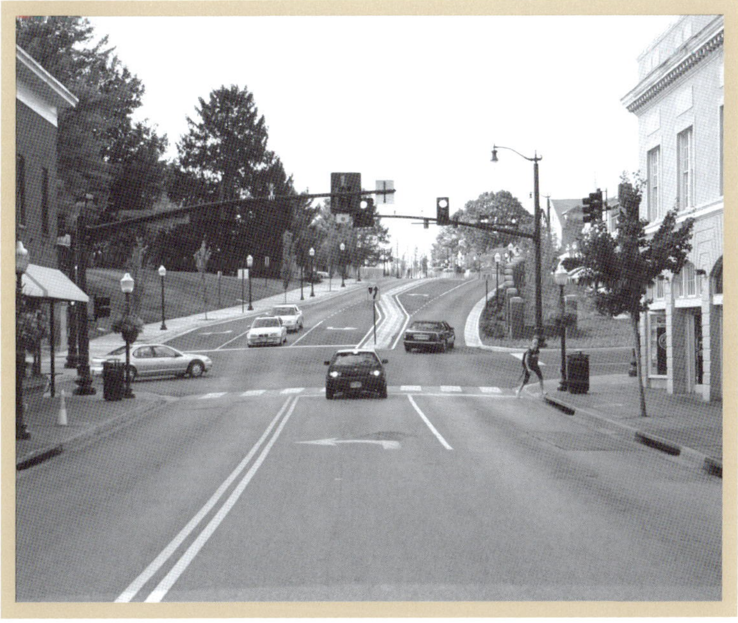

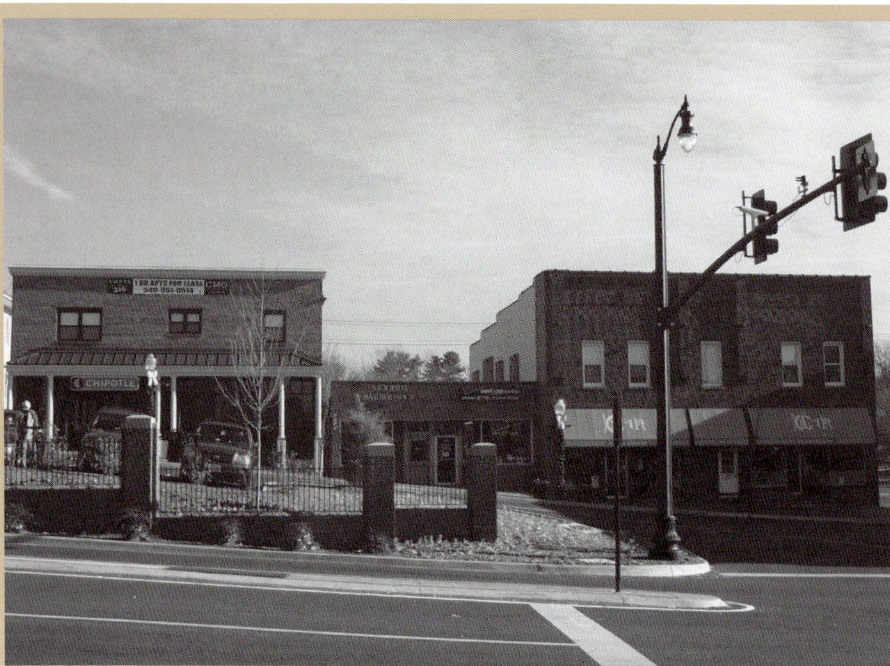

College Avenue Extension is the jog in Main Street that once went around the Preston and Olin Institute. This 1950s photograph shows the buildings much as they are today. Businesses included a laundry, television and photographic services, Modern Barber Shop, Blue Ribbon Restaurant, and a billiard parlor. Modern Barber Shop remains, while the other buildings now house Chipotle, a Verizon Wireless store, and The Cellar Restaurant. (TOB.)

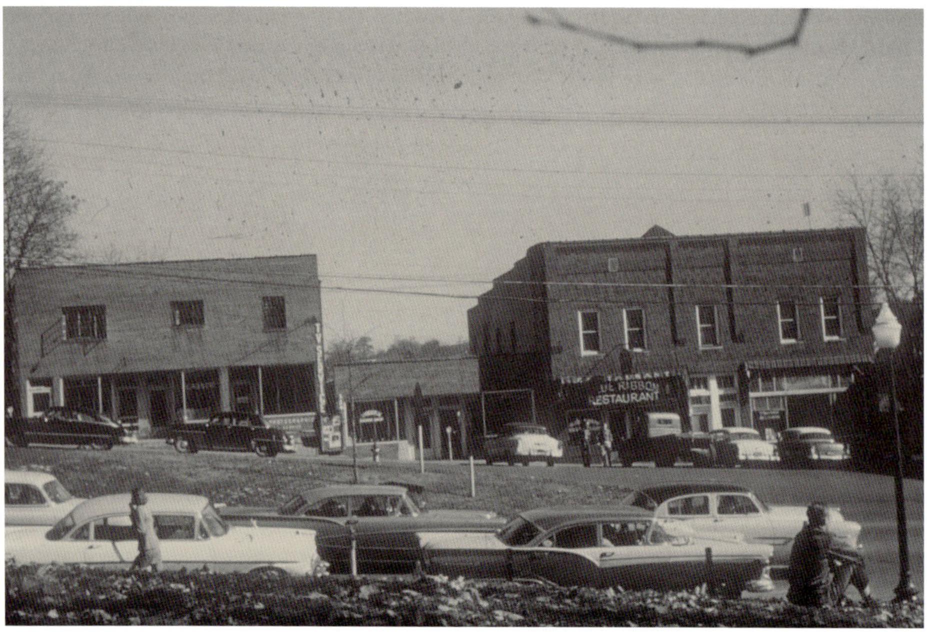

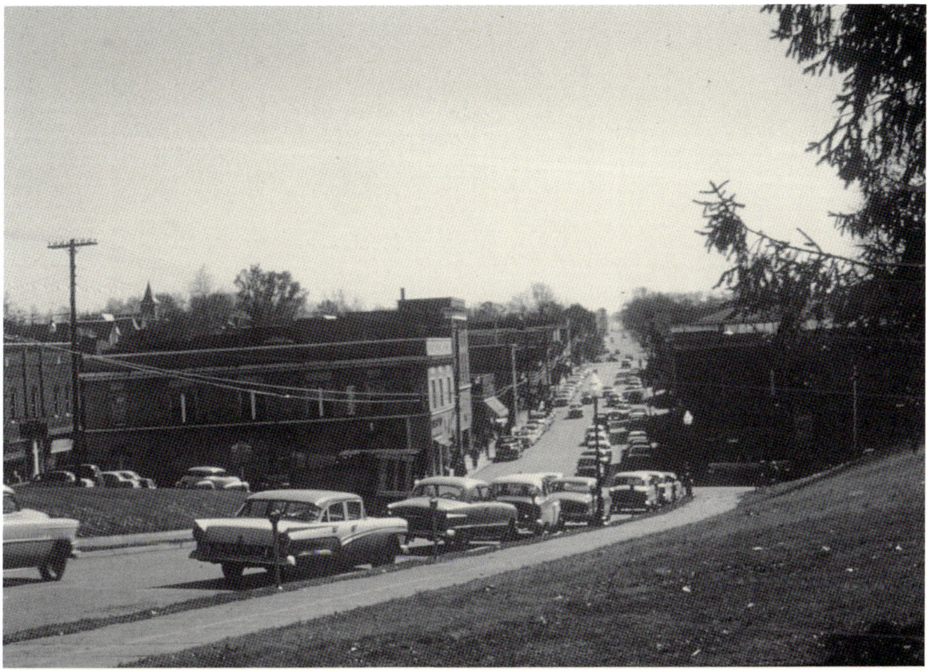

This 1950s view up South Main Street from Henderson Lawn through the College Avenue intersection shows the busy downtown area. This photograph was taken near where the Preston and Olin Institute building caused the jog in Main Street, visible to the left. (TOB.)

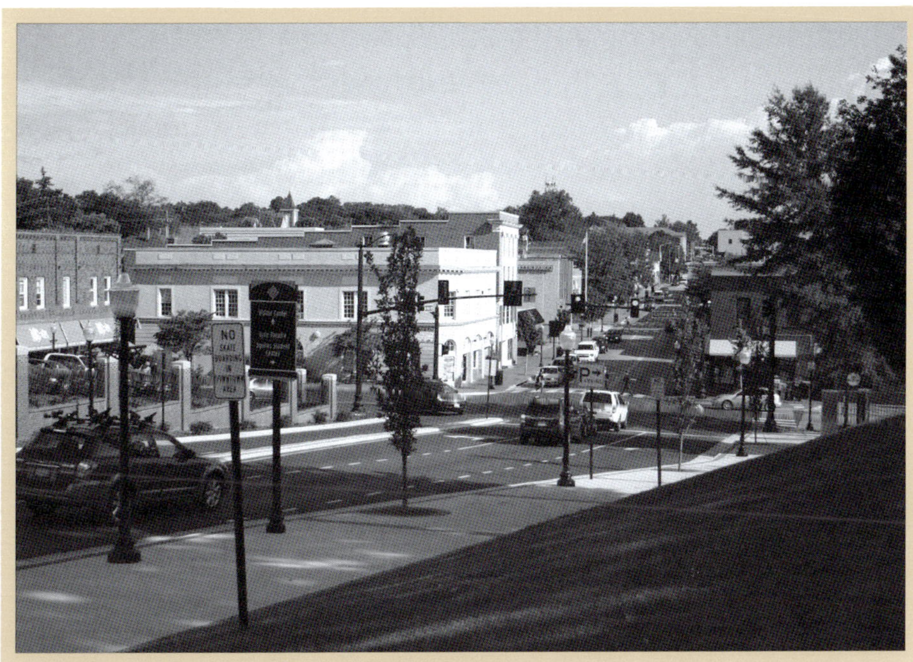

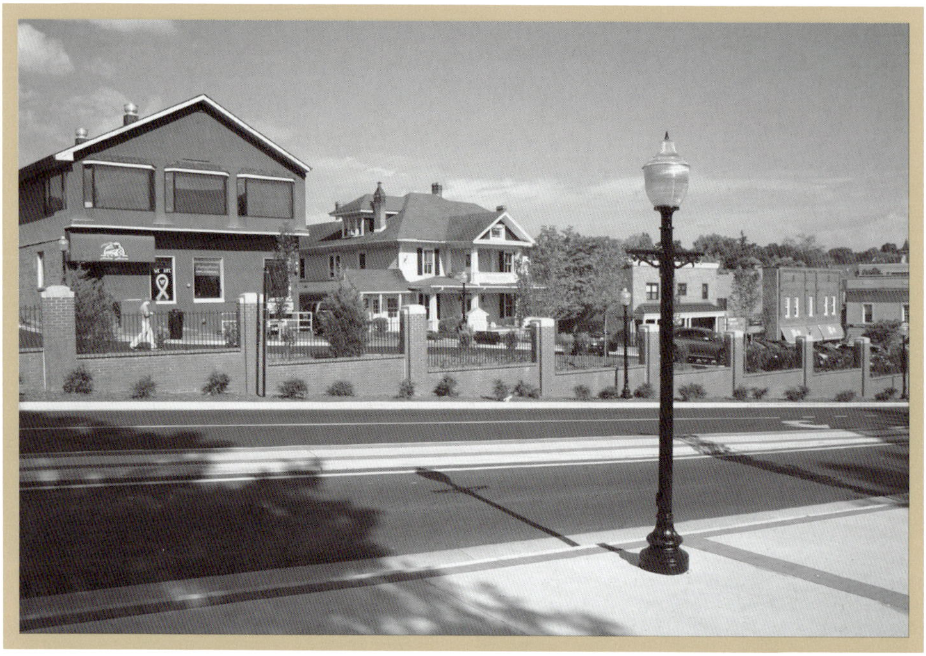

North Main Street above the College Avenue intersection is undergoing renovations to make the street pedestrian-friendly again. While Main Street will not have parallel parking, new brick walls, a median, and wider sidewalks are narrowing lanes to slow traffic. The College Avenue Extension in front of the buildings is no longer a through street, but instead provides patio space outside for the restaurants to add tables. (TOB.)

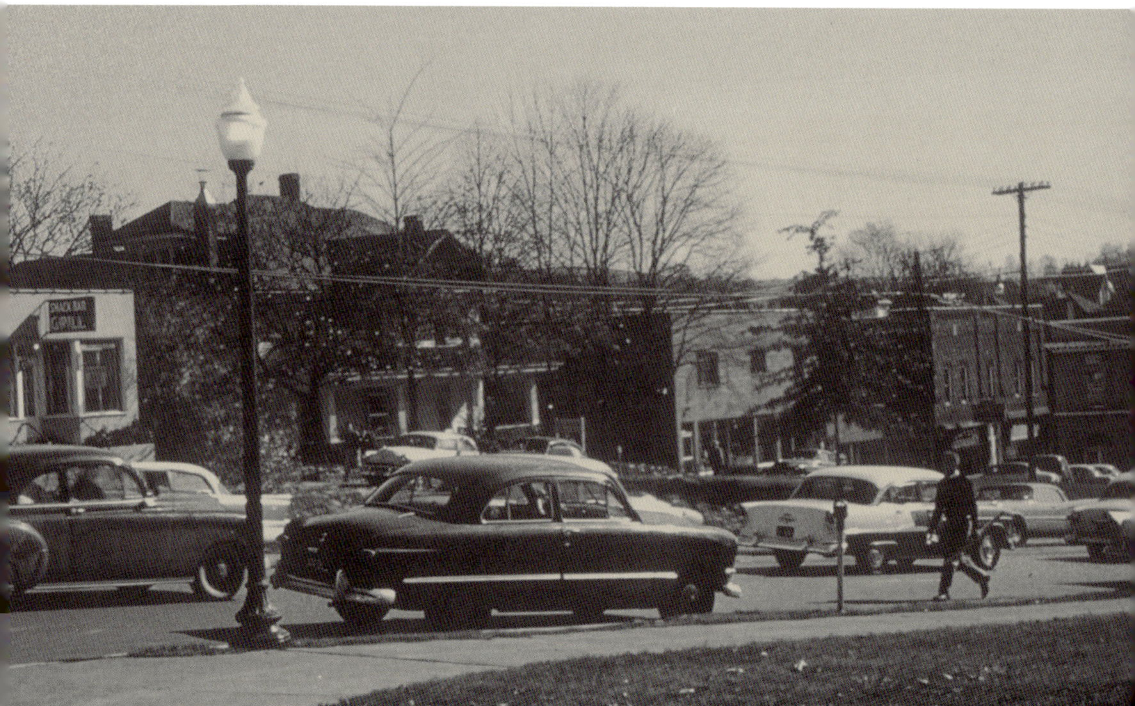

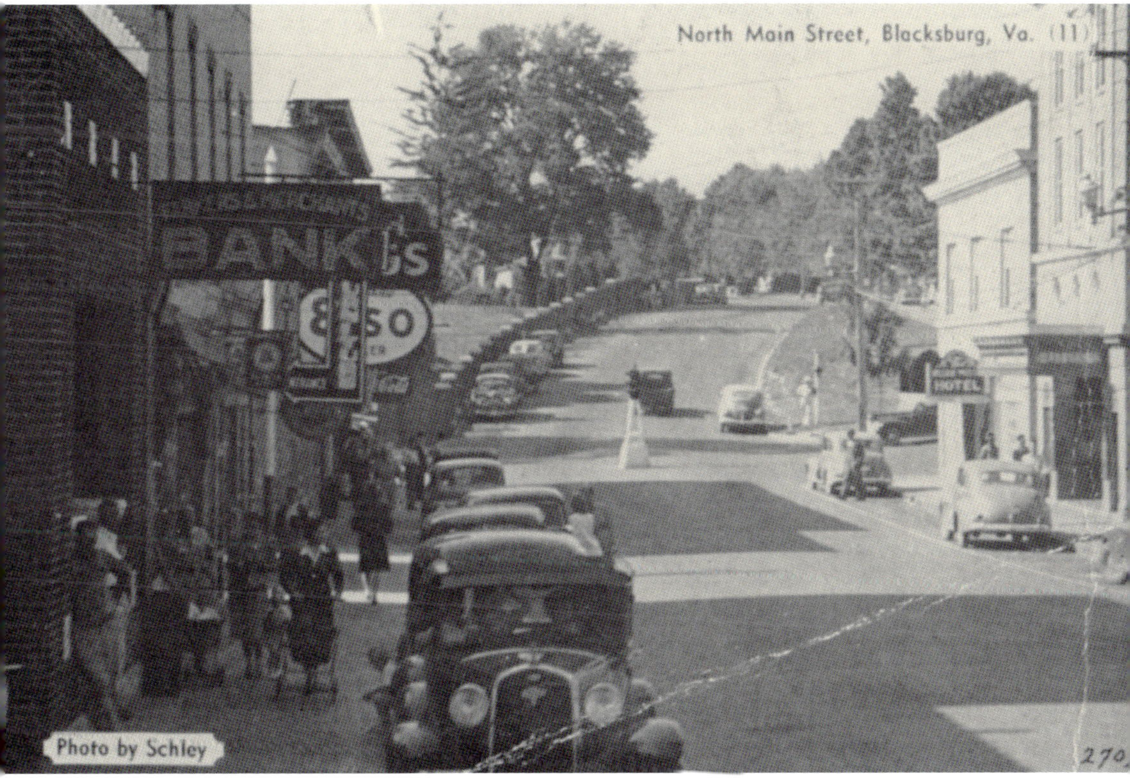

This 1930s photograph of the intersection of North Main Street and College Avenue shows a bank, a gas station, a drugstore, and a hotel. Today, restaurants, clothing stores, and specialty shops fill these same buildings, providing an entirely different shopping experience. Also important to note is the on-street parallel parking, which has given way to an extra lane of traffic. (DLA.)

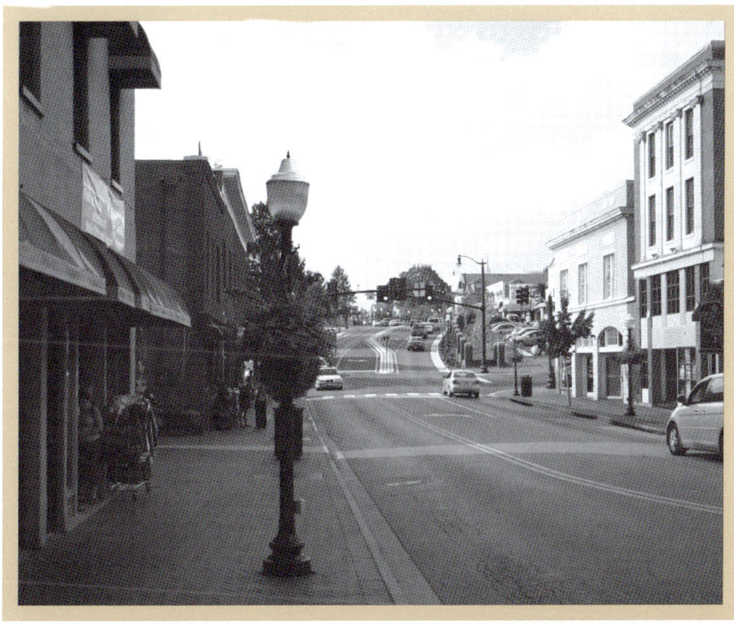

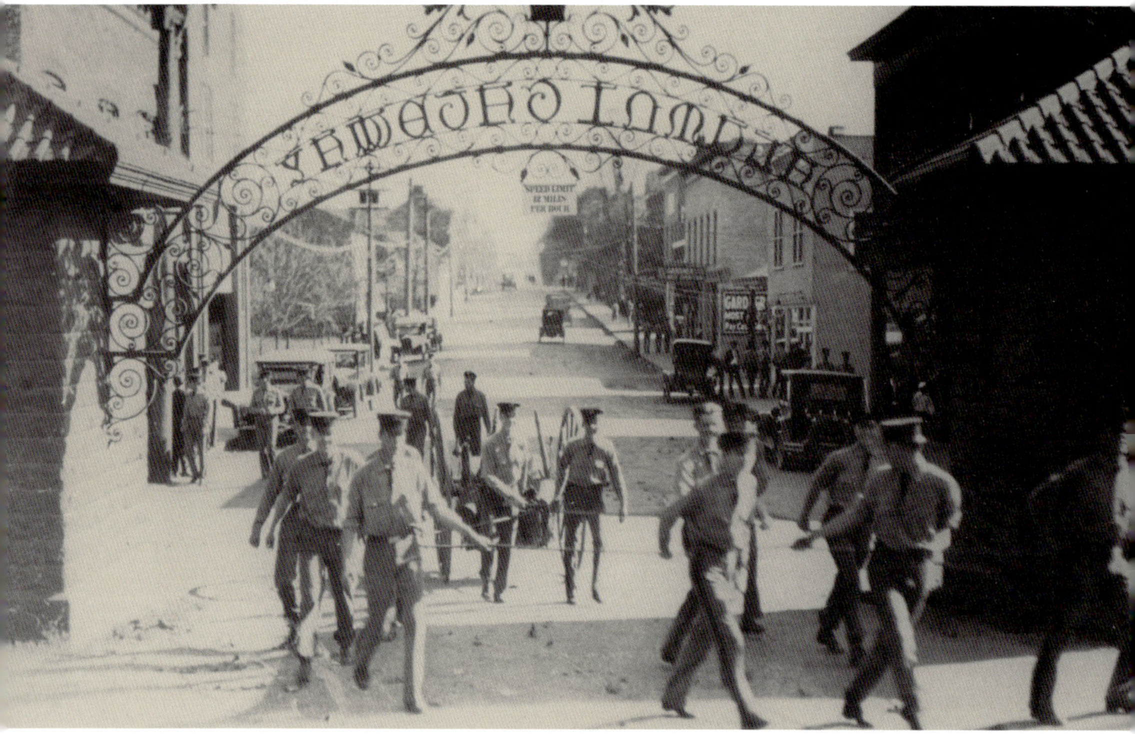

The Alumni Gateway was constructed at the intersection of College Avenue and Main Street during the 1913–1914 school year to mark the entrance to campus. A curving road traveled from the gateway up the hill by Henderson Hall and through the upper quad near Lane Hall. The gateway witnessed many parades of cadets, including this one in the 1920s. Note the 12 miles per hour speed limit posted below it. The gateway was removed in 1936 when Main Street was widened. (DLA.)

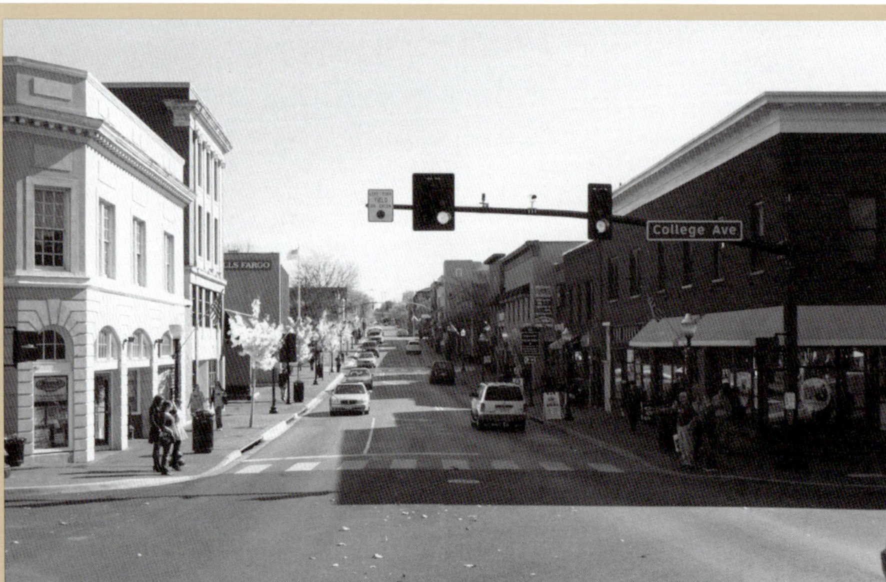

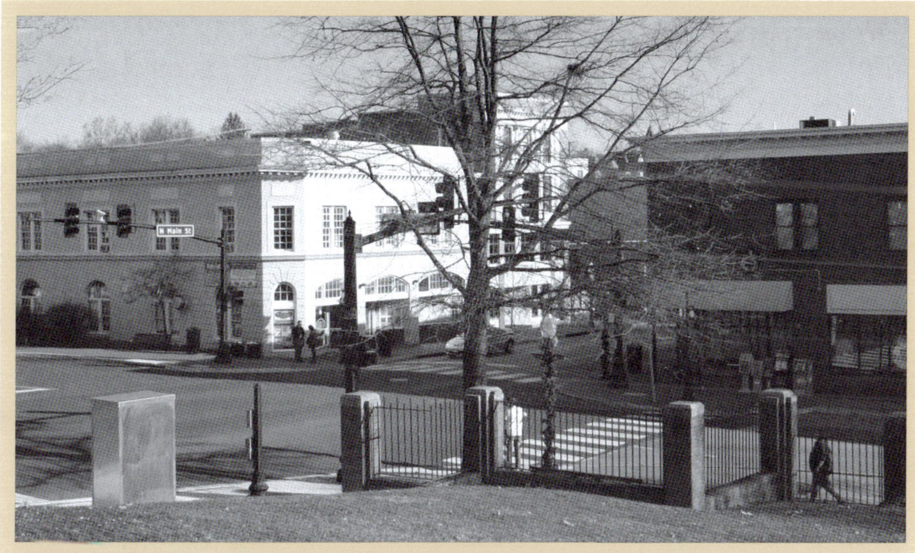

A parade is shown passing through the old Alumni Gateway at the intersection of Main Street and College Avenue in the early 1920s. The parade headed onto campus on the driveway through what is now Henderson Lawn. The J.H. Woolwine store no longer exists, but the Ellett Building, also known as the Preston Hotel, still does. Today, Sharkey's Restaurant is on the first floor and apartments are above. (DLA.)

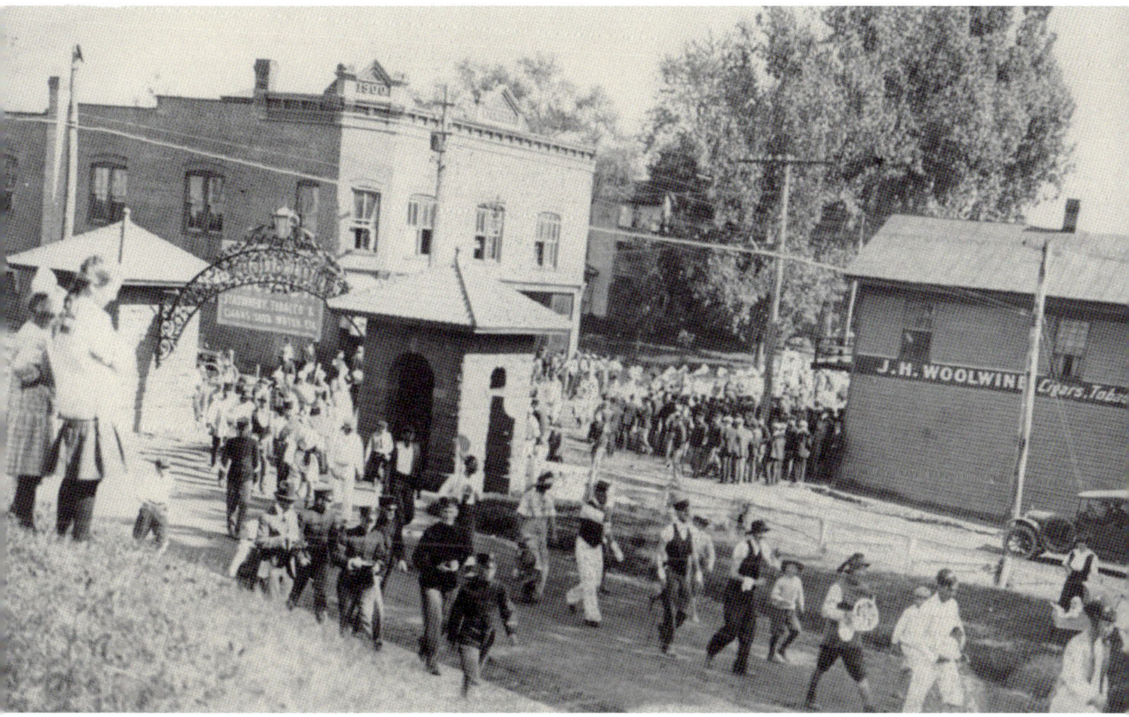

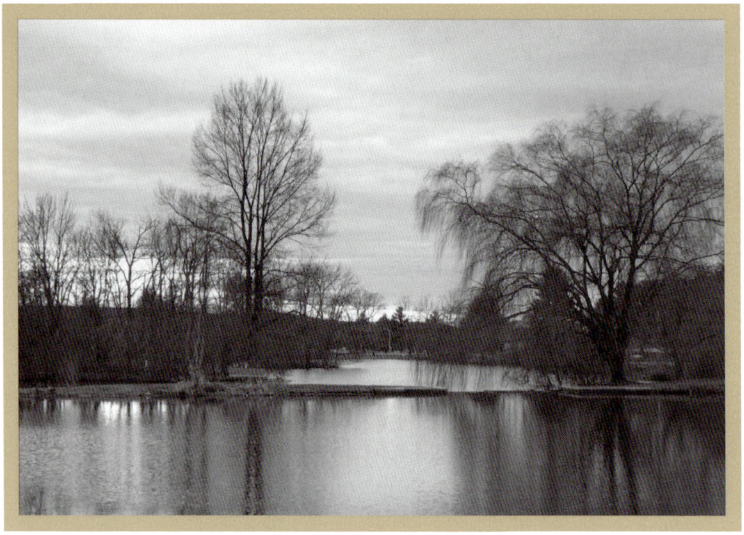

Blacksburg is a town of many springs, creeks, and tributaries. Because it has been piped underground in many places, most people do not realize that Strouble's Creek runs from downtown Blacksburg, under the Drillfield, to the Duck Pond before traveling out through Hethwood to the New River. Strouble's Creek was dammed in the 1930s to create the Duck Pond, a popular place for parents and children, picnics, duck feeding, romantic strolls, and studying. (DLA.)

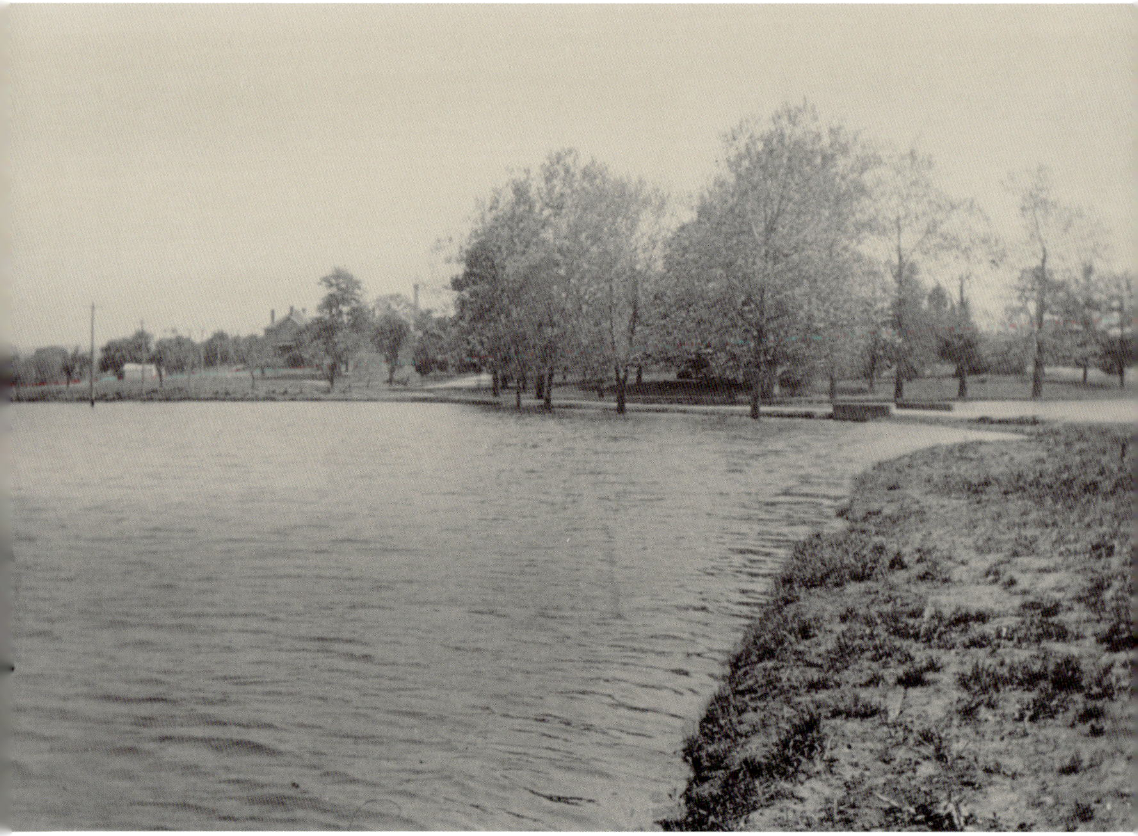

CHAPTER 7

CAMPUS

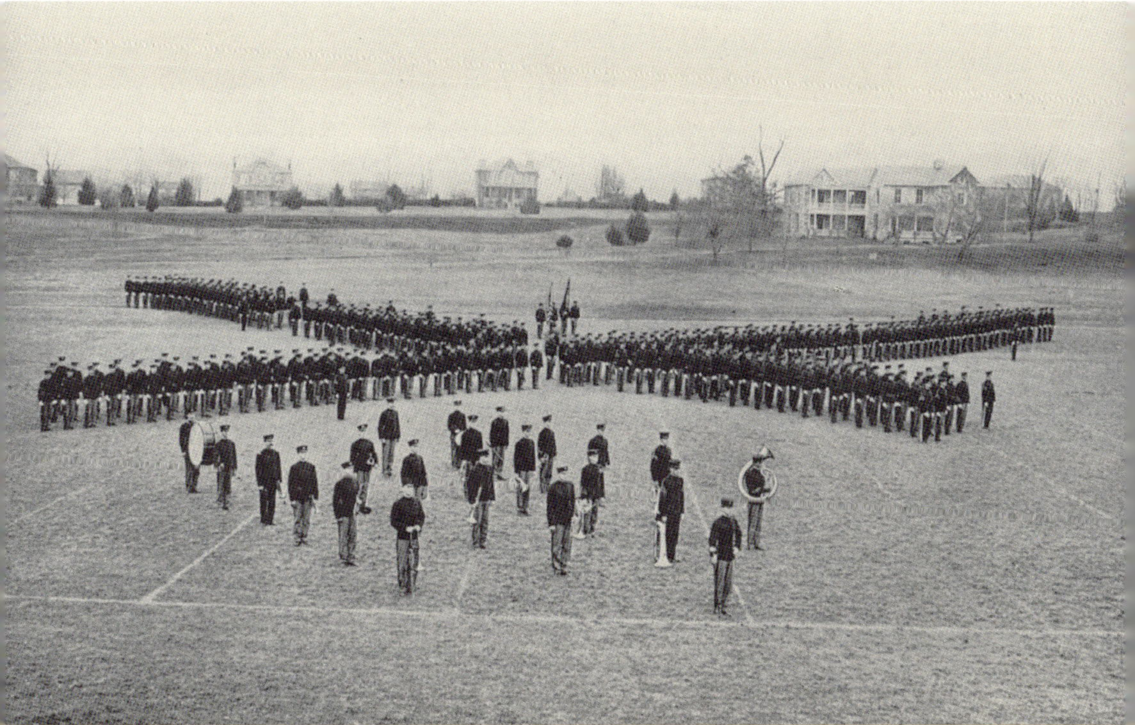

When Virginia Agricultural and Mechanical College was founded in 1872, all students were cadets. The Drillfield became the center of campus and the location of Corps of Cadets activities in 1894. Virginia Tech has grown immensely since this photograph was taken in the early 1900s, but the Drillfield and Cadet Corps are still important elements of campus. (DLA.)

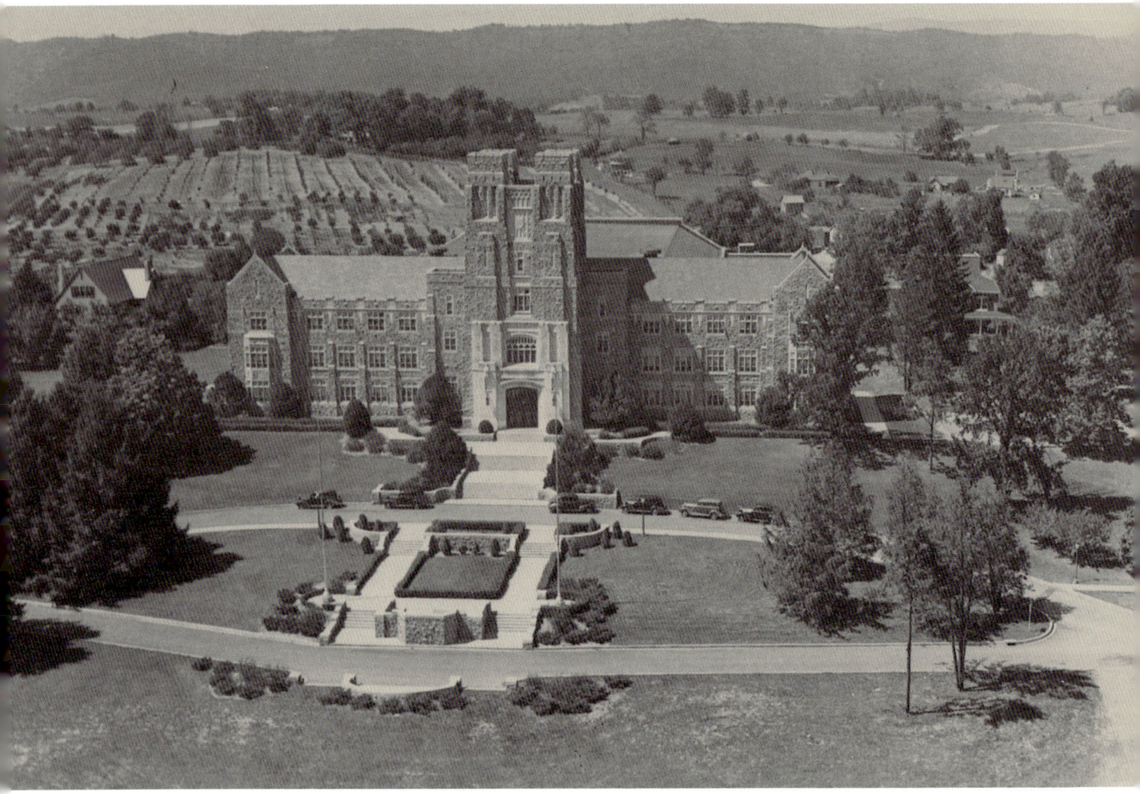

Burruss Hall was completed in 1936 with grant funding from the Works Progress Administration (WPA). Originally called the Teaching and Administration Building, Burruss Hall replaced the earlier administration building on another section of the Drillfield. Overlooking the Drillfield, Burruss Hall is the iconic view of the Virginia Tech campus and is still home to the president's office, other administrative offices, and the largest auditorium on campus. (DLA.)

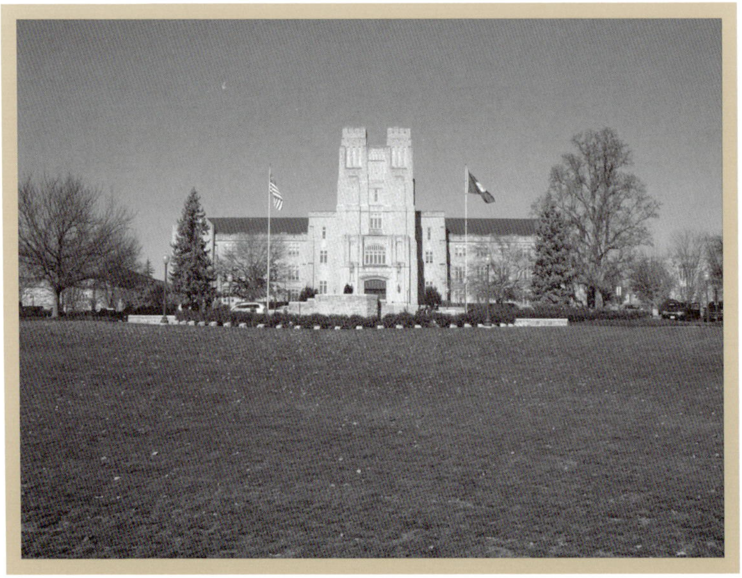

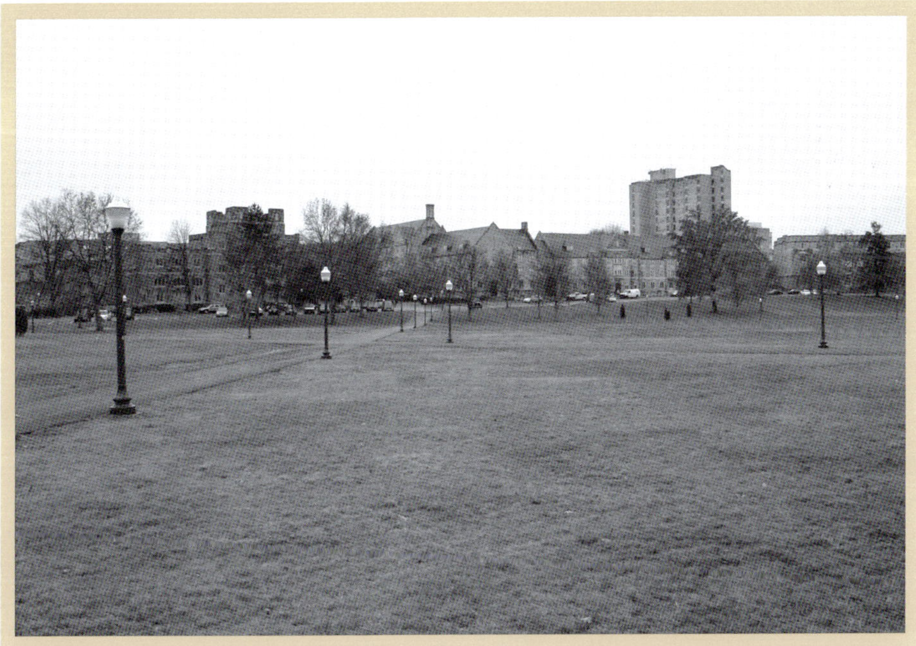

This view of the Drillfield from around 1933 shows World War I Memorial Gymnasium at center and Barracks No. 8 to the right. A water tower is visible on the knoll to the rear. The buildings have been renamed War Memorial Hall and Campbell Hall and have grown and changed as the student population has expanded. The knoll behind is now filled with dormitories, and the well-traversed paths of the Drillfield have been paved and lighted. (DLA.)

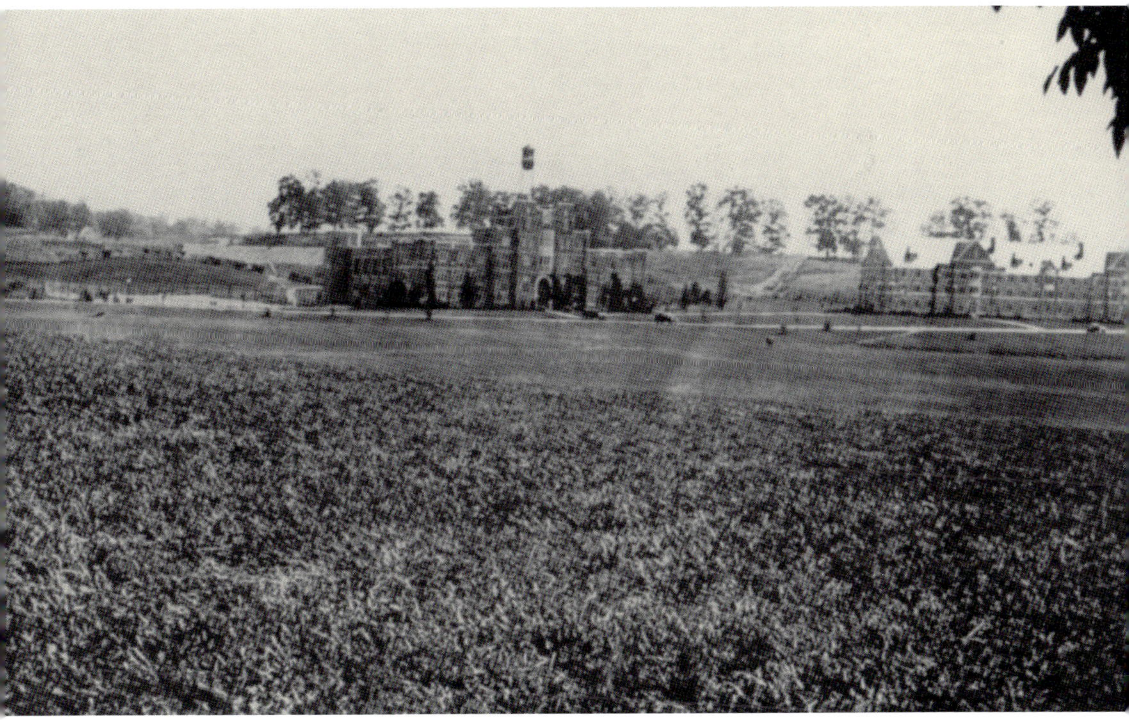

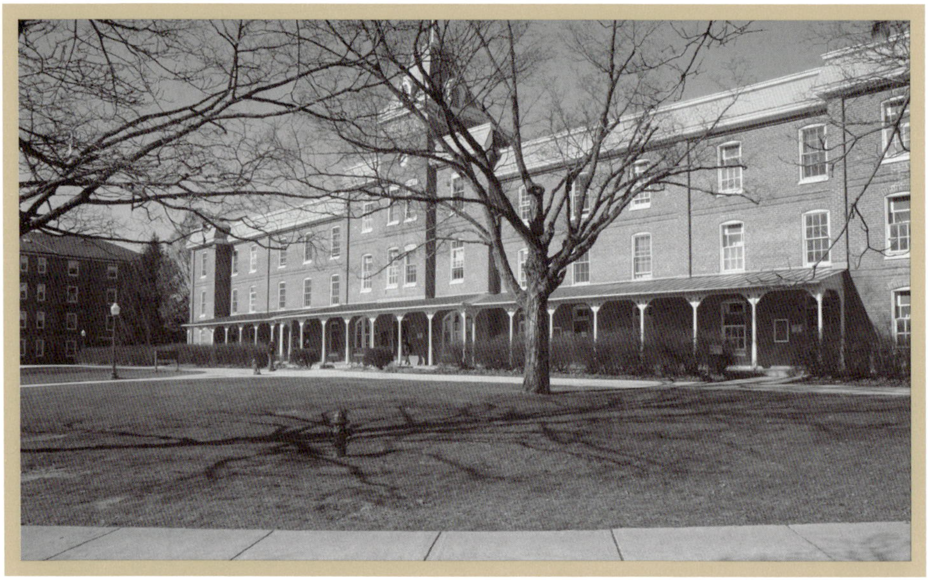

Lane Hall is one of the oldest remaining academic buildings on the Virginia Tech campus. The building is named for Confederate general James H. Lane, the first commandant of the Virginia Tech Corps of Cadets. As it was the first dormitory for cadets, it was known as Barracks No. 1. When it was built in 1888, its bathrooms were considered revolutionary as they featured hot and cold running water. Today, the building holds the offices of the College of Liberal Arts and Human Studies. (DLA.)

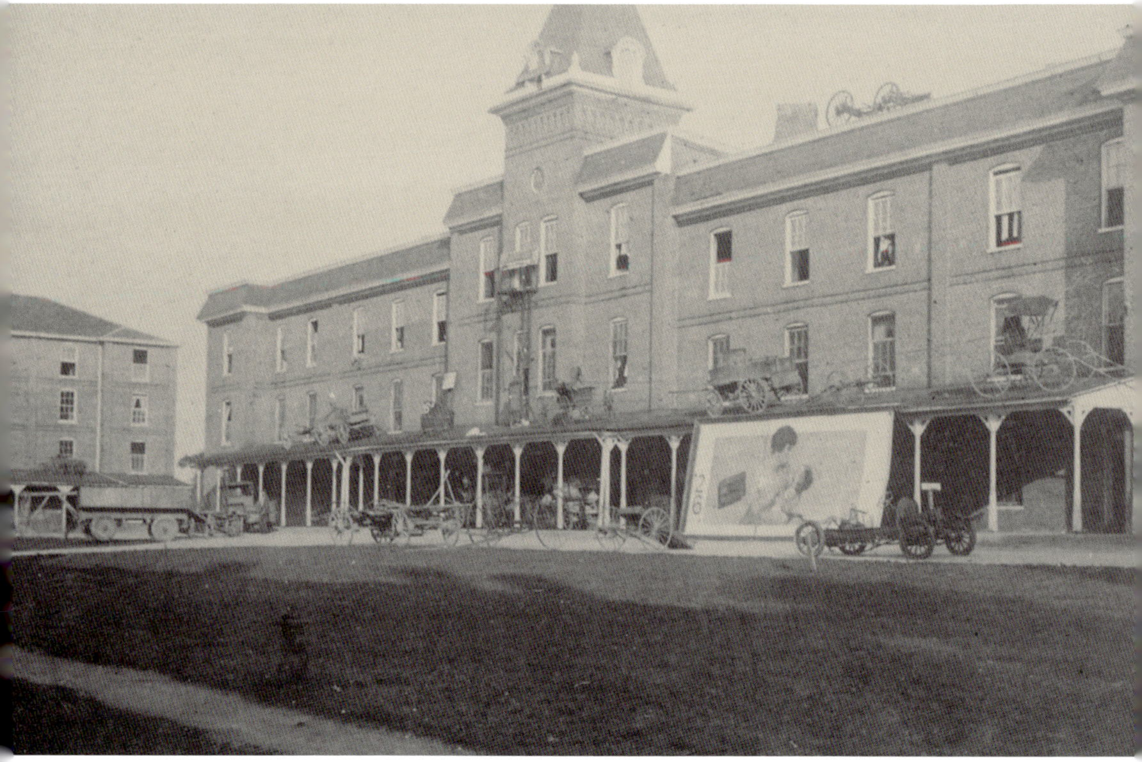

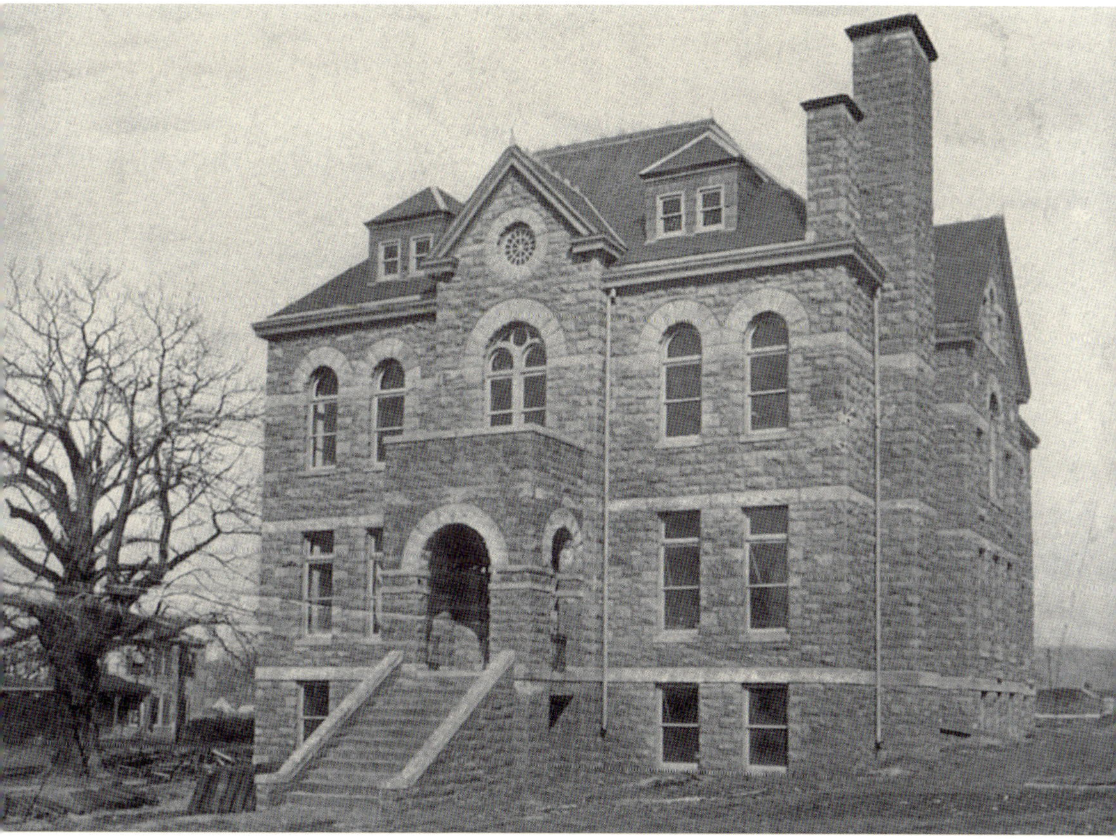

The Romanesque Performing Arts Building was originally constructed by the YMCA in 1899. Privately funded, it was the first building on the Virginia Tech campus made of the local limestone that has come to be called Hokie Stone. The YMCA moved from the building in 1937 and gave it to Virginia Tech in 1972. The YMCA at Virginia Tech is still a strong presence in Blacksburg but is now located off campus. (DLA.)

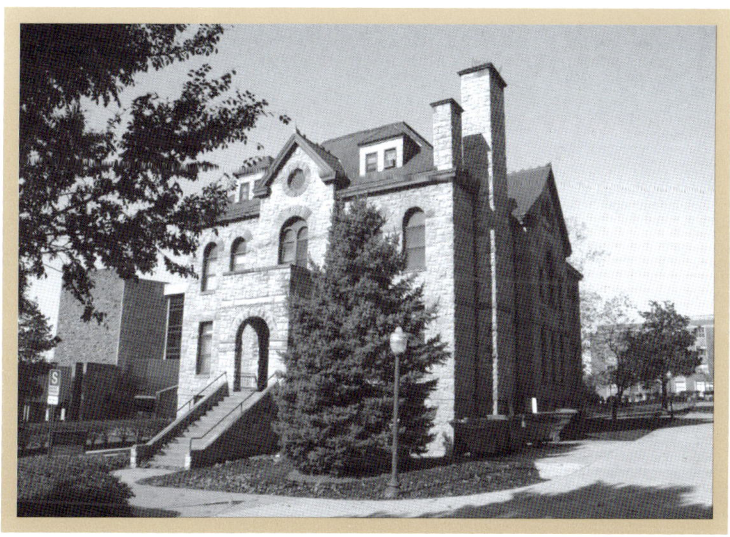

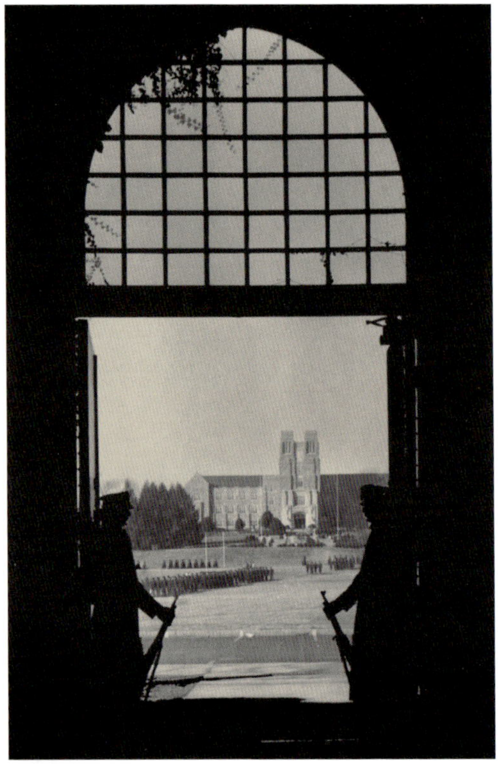

War Memorial Hall sits directly across the Drillfield from Burruss Hall. The building contains a gymnasium financed by alumni contributions to memorialize Virginia Tech lives lost in World War I. The varsity basketball team played in the gym from 1926 to 1961. Today, in addition to academic offices, the Virginia Tech community uses War Memorial Hall's gym and swimming pool. (DLA.)

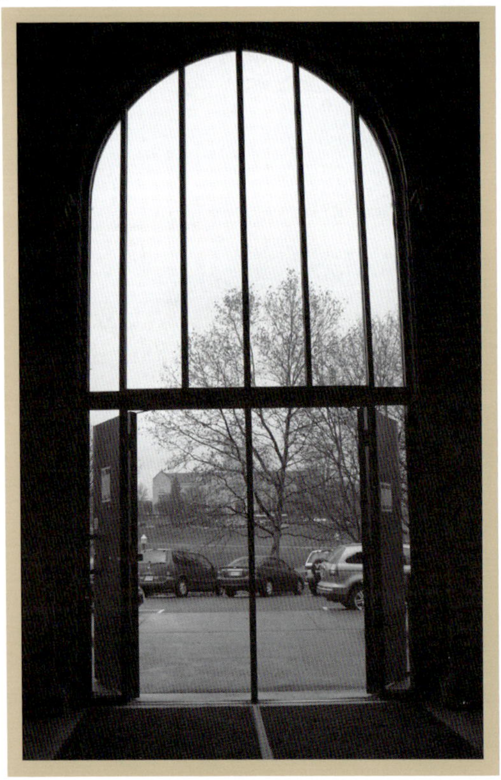

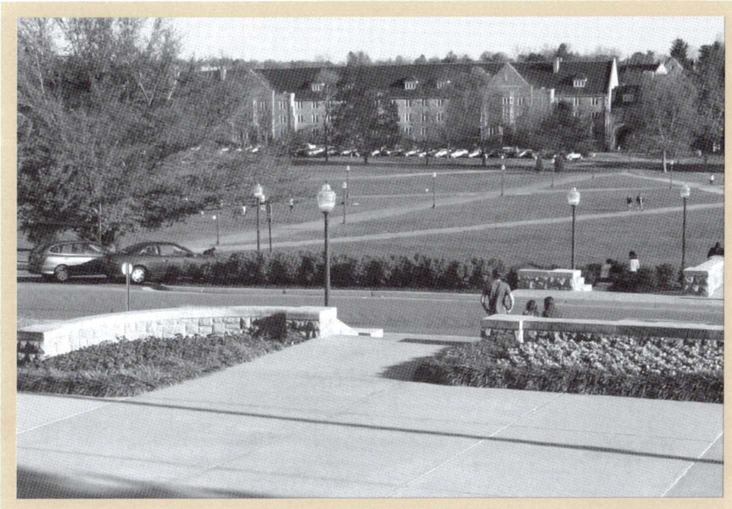

The view from the steps of Burruss Hall in this historical photograph shows the Corps of Cadets in formation on the Drillfield and a road configuration slightly different than today. Directly in front of Burruss Hall, an impromptu memorial was created by students, faculty, and staff in the wake of the tragic shootings of April 16, 2007. The memorial has since been made permanent, with a semicircle of Hokie Stones engraved with the names of each of the 32 victims. (JK.)

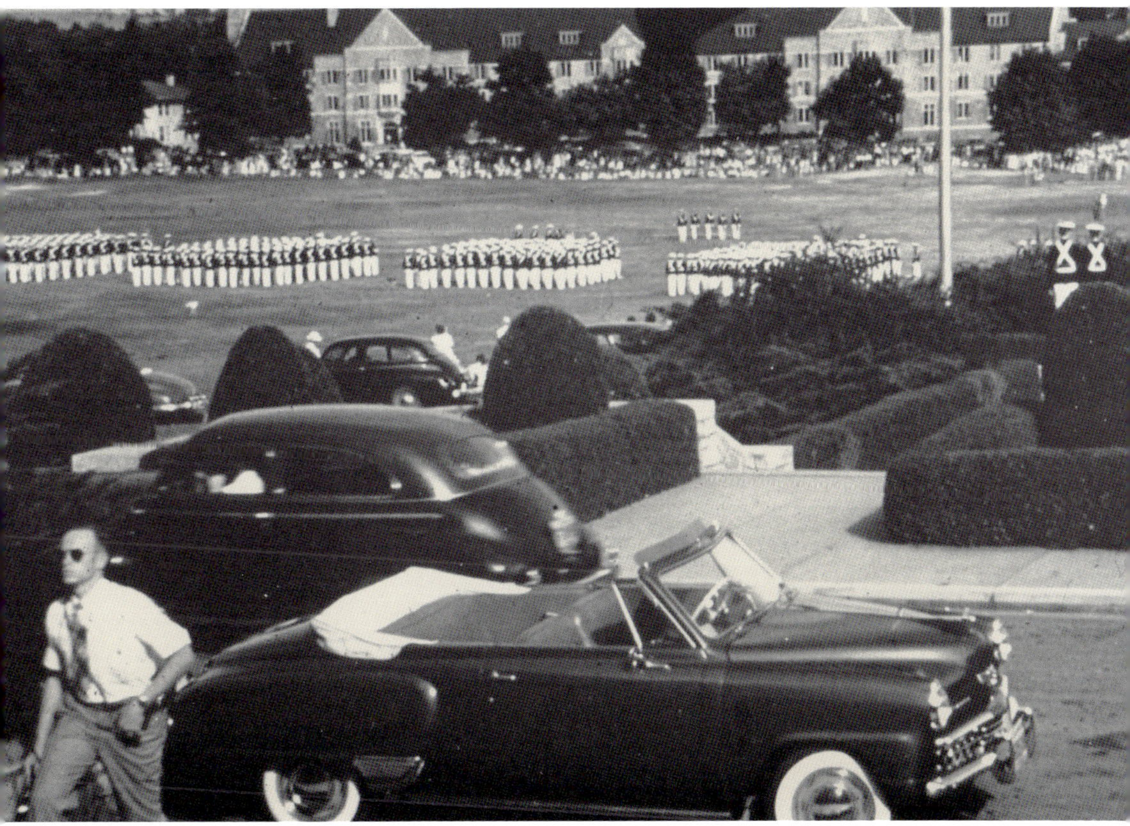

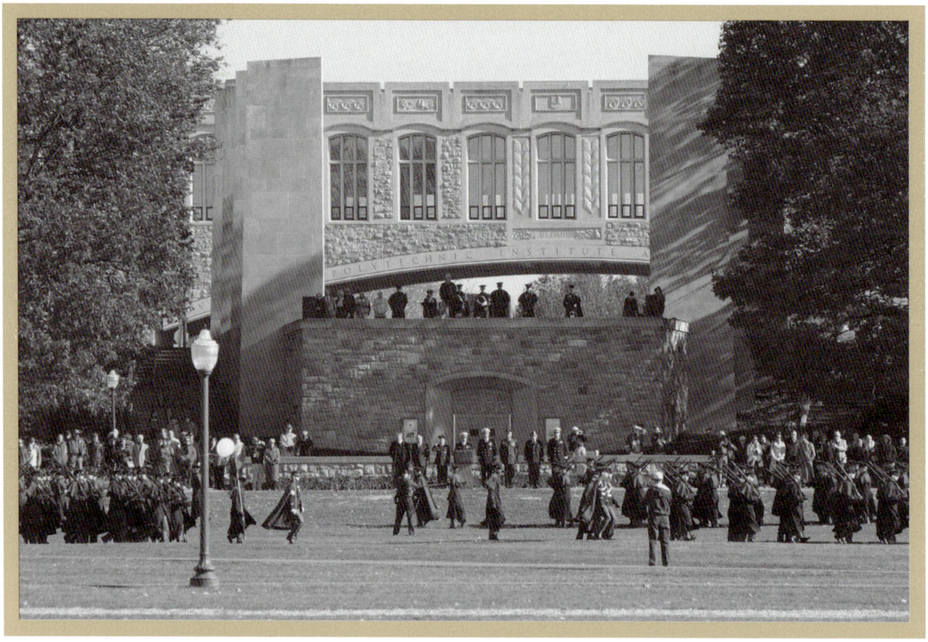

The Corps of Cadets march in review on the Drillfield in front of War Memorial Chapel. The chapel was completed in 1960 to honor alumni lost in World War II. Today, the chapel also honors those lost in wars since. The Torgersen Hall Bridge is in the background of the current photograph, crossing the Alumni Mall to connect Torgersen Hall to the Carol M. Newman Library. (DLA.)

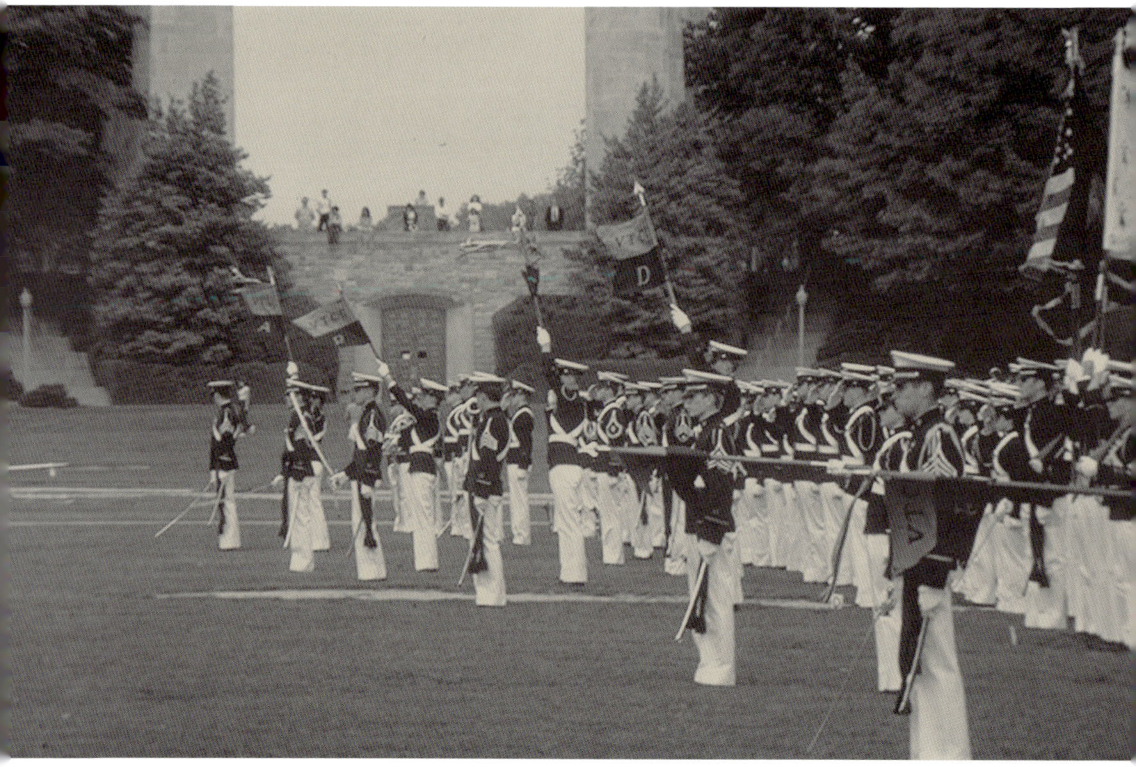

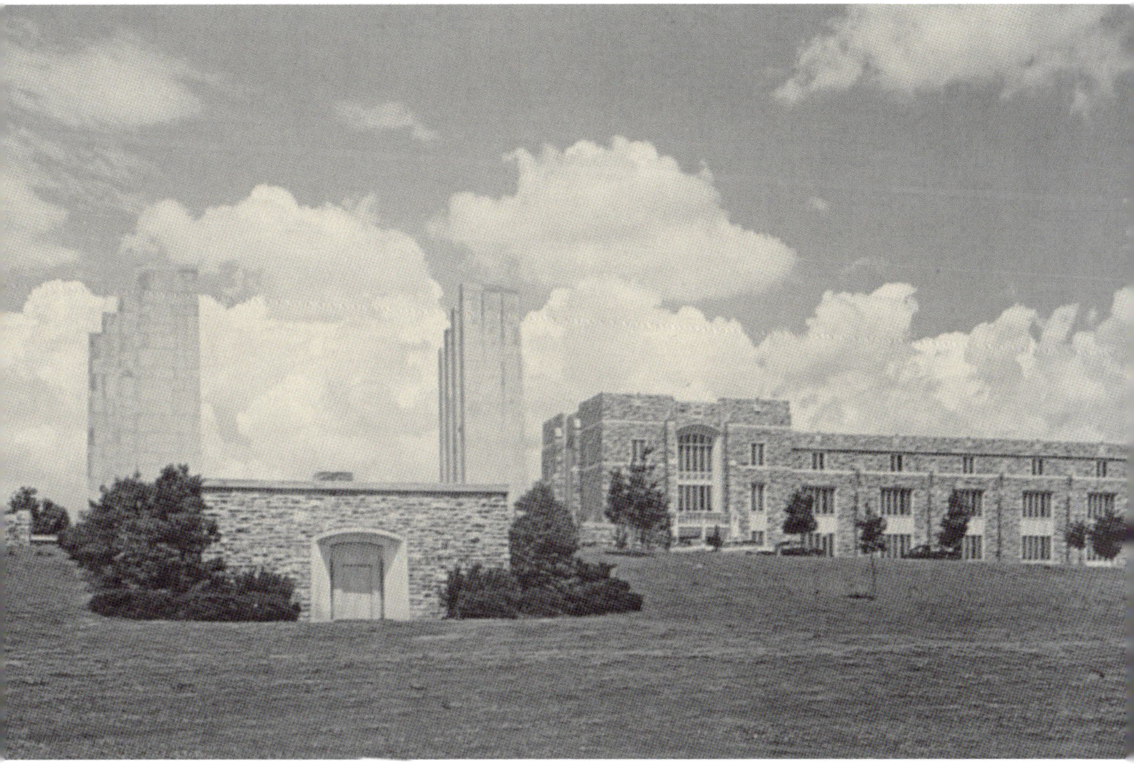

This view shows the War Memorial Chapel to the left and the Carol M. Newman Library to the right. Construction of the chapel began in 1951 and was completed in 1960. The upper-level Memorial Court has eight limestone pylons representing Brotherhood, Honor, Leadership, Sacrifice, Service, Loyalty, Duty, and Ut Prosim—"That I May Serve"—with the names of alumni servicemen and women who have lost their lives in military service. The lower level contains a 260-seat chapel. (TOB.)

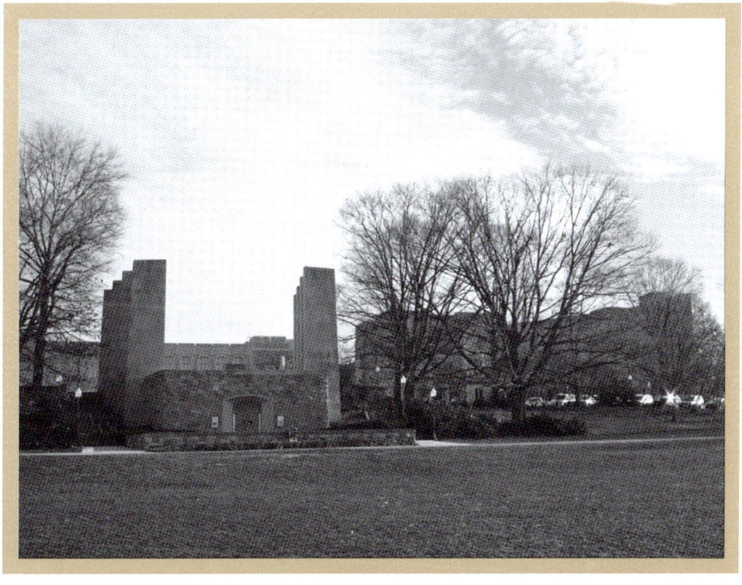

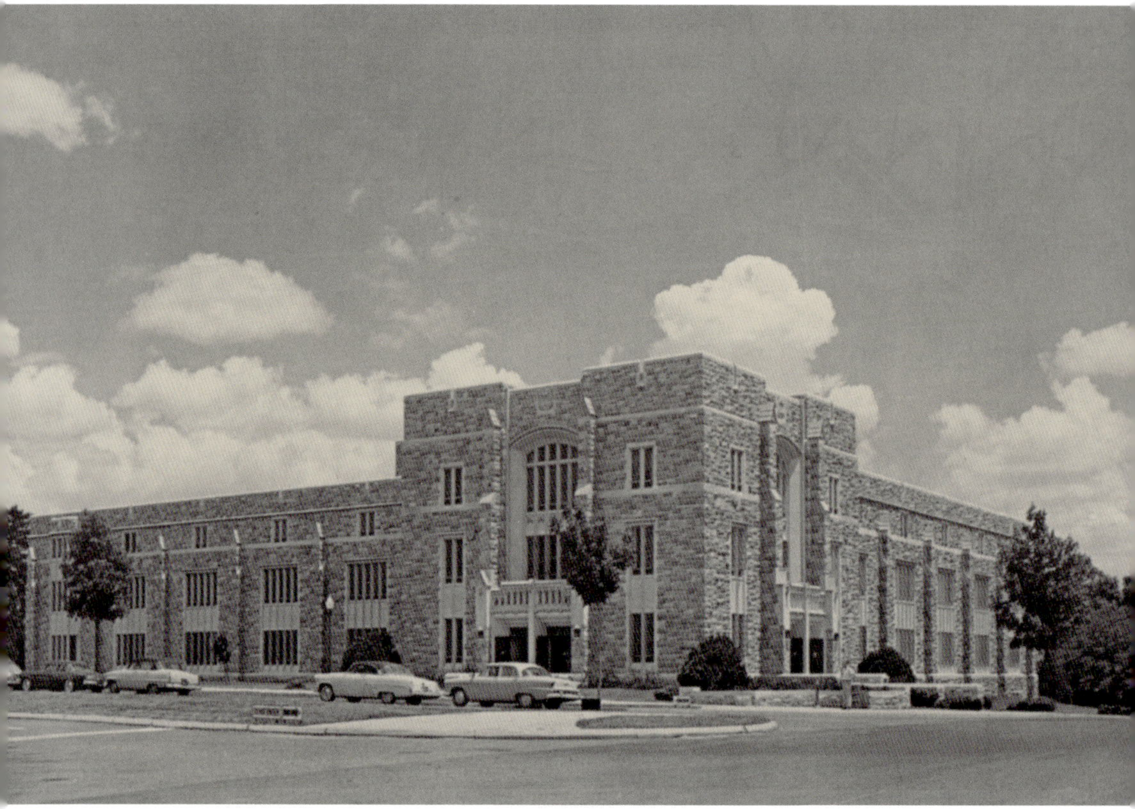

Virginia Tech's library was established in 1872 with 500 volumes and was housed in an academic building. The Carol M. Newman Library opened in 1955 near the site of the chapel. A six-story addition, visible to the right in the modern photograph, was completed in 1981. Torgerson Hall was connected to the library in 2000. Today, Virginia Tech's library system includes more than two million volumes as well as electronic holdings and digital images of local history. (TOB.)

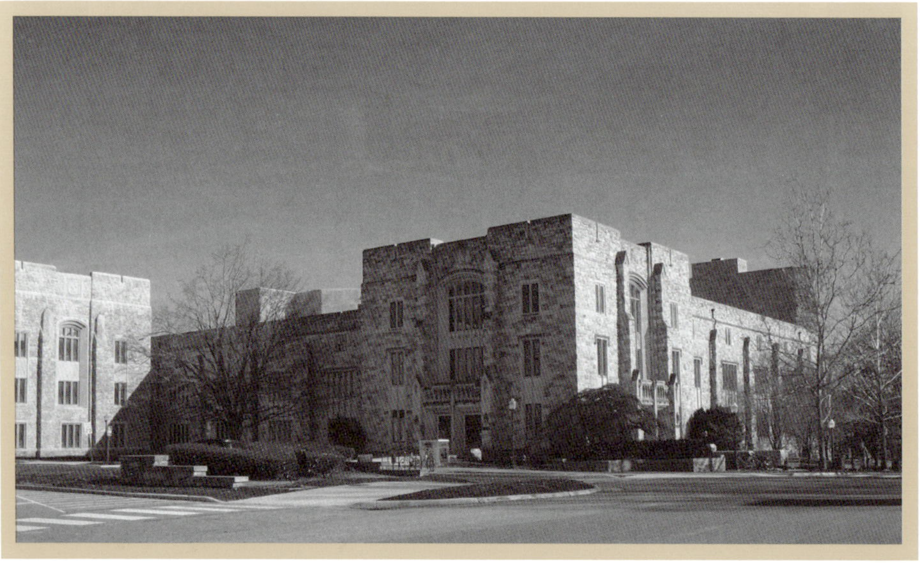

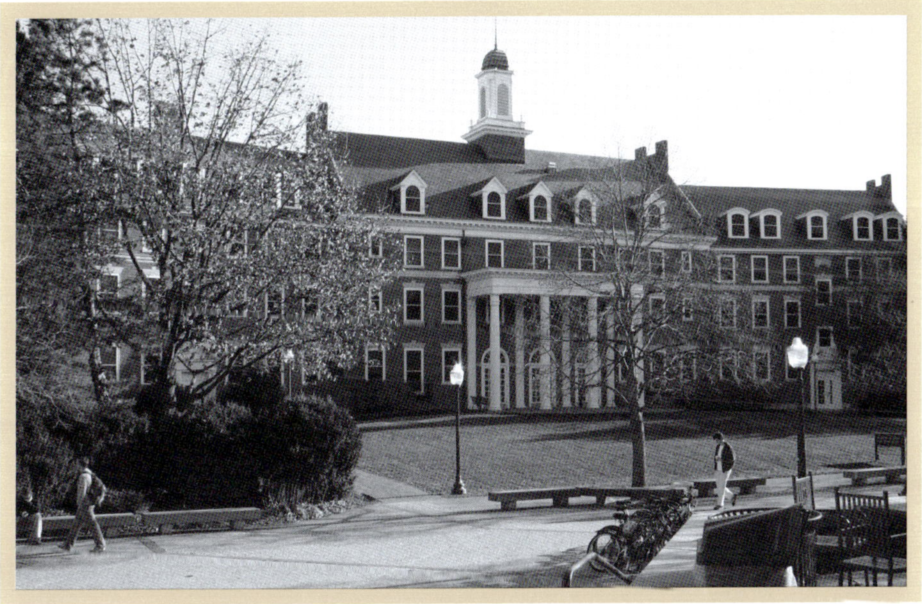

The Graduate Life Center at Donaldson Brown was built in 1935 as the Faculty Center, an apartment house and dining hall for faculty members. When it was constructed, Blacksburg businesses were concerned that the building would ruin property values. After the addition of an auditorium, large dining room, and conference rooms in the 1960s, the building became the university's hotel and conference center. Today, the building contains graduate offices and dormitories. (DLA.)

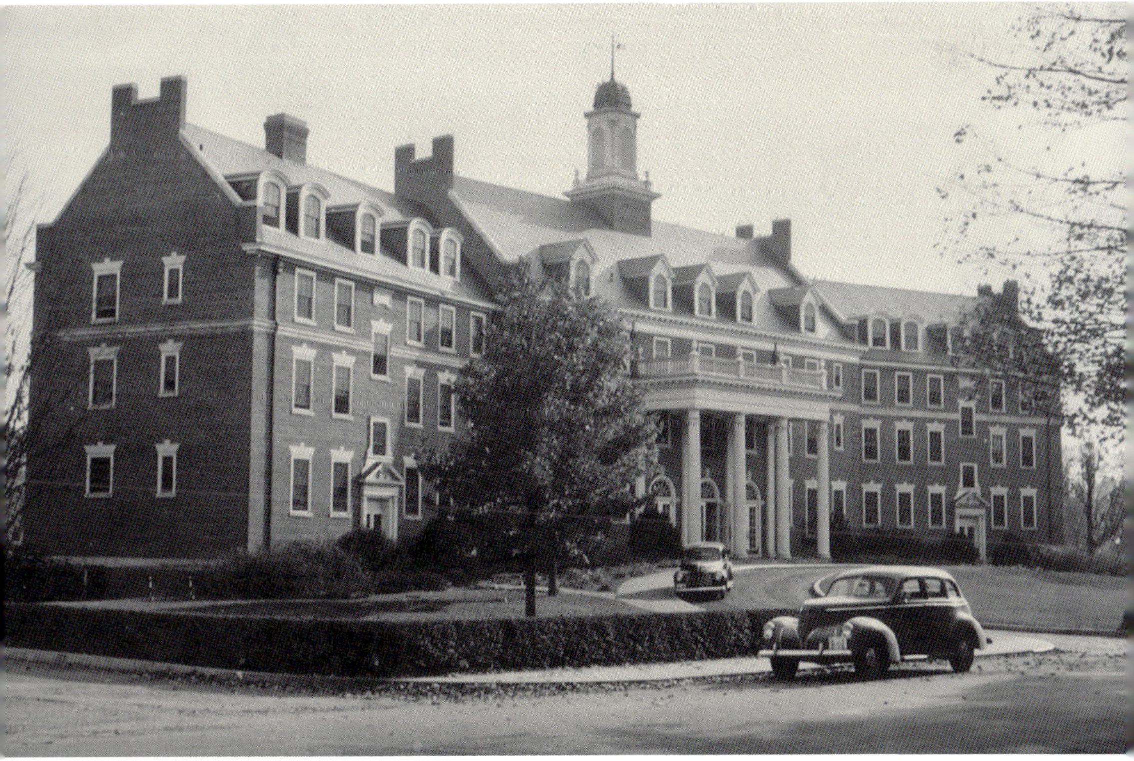

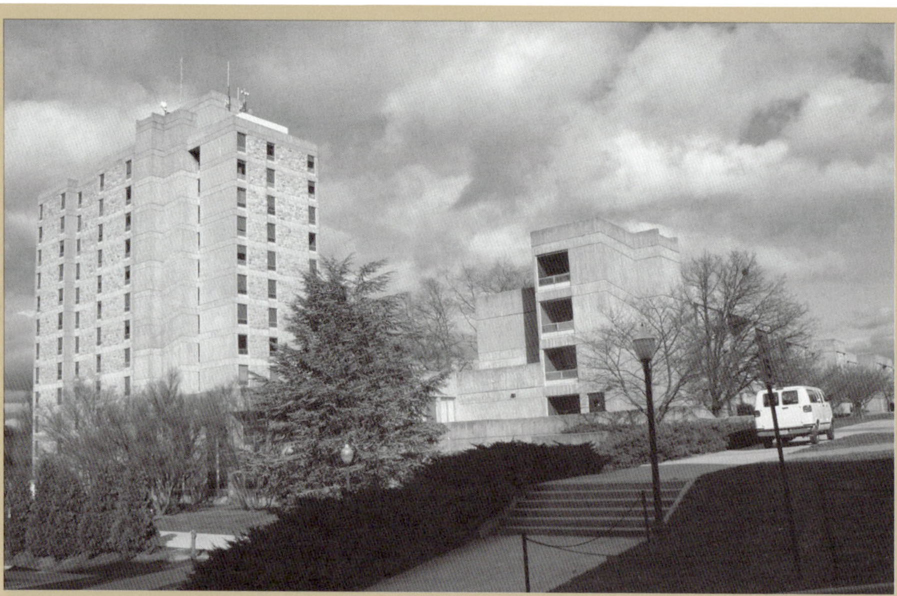

Slusher Tower was completed in 1972 and, at 12 stories high, has the most floors of any building on campus. Combined with Slusher Wing, to the right, Slusher Hall is home to over 600 undergraduates in the Drillfield community. The building is named for Clarice Slusher Pritchard, a 1927 alumna of Virginia Tech who worked as assistant registrar for nearly 40 years. (DLA.)

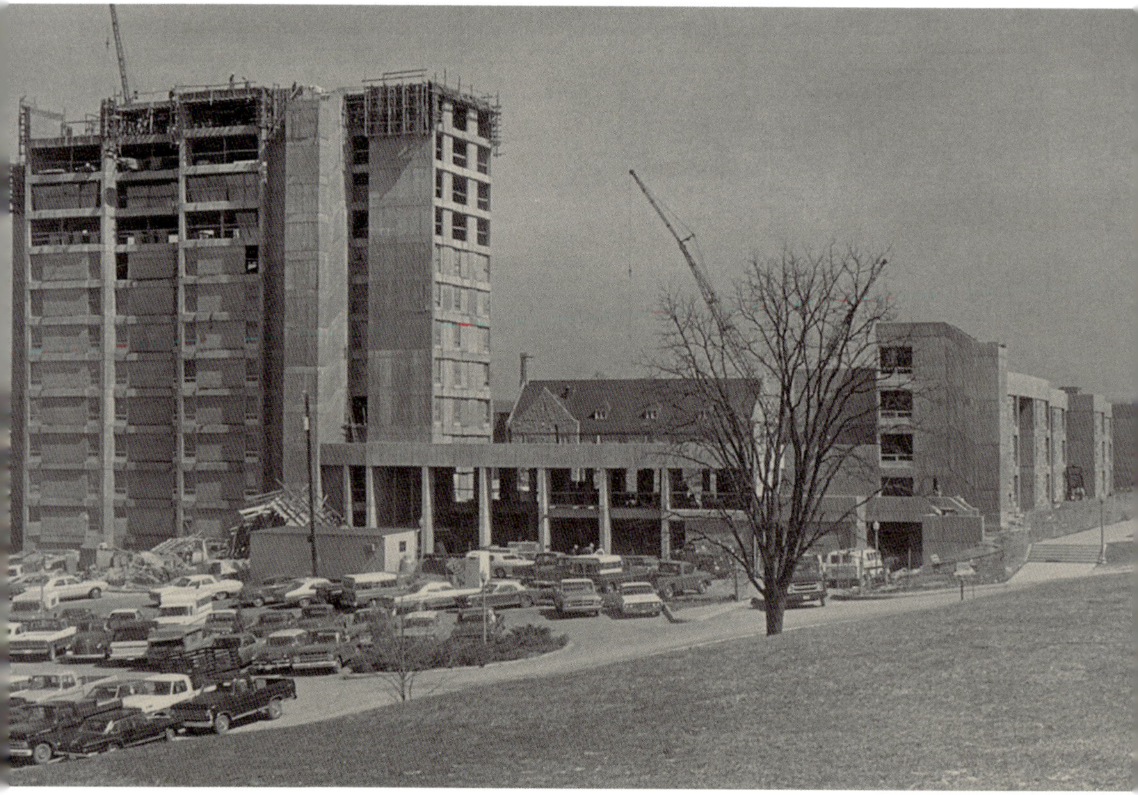

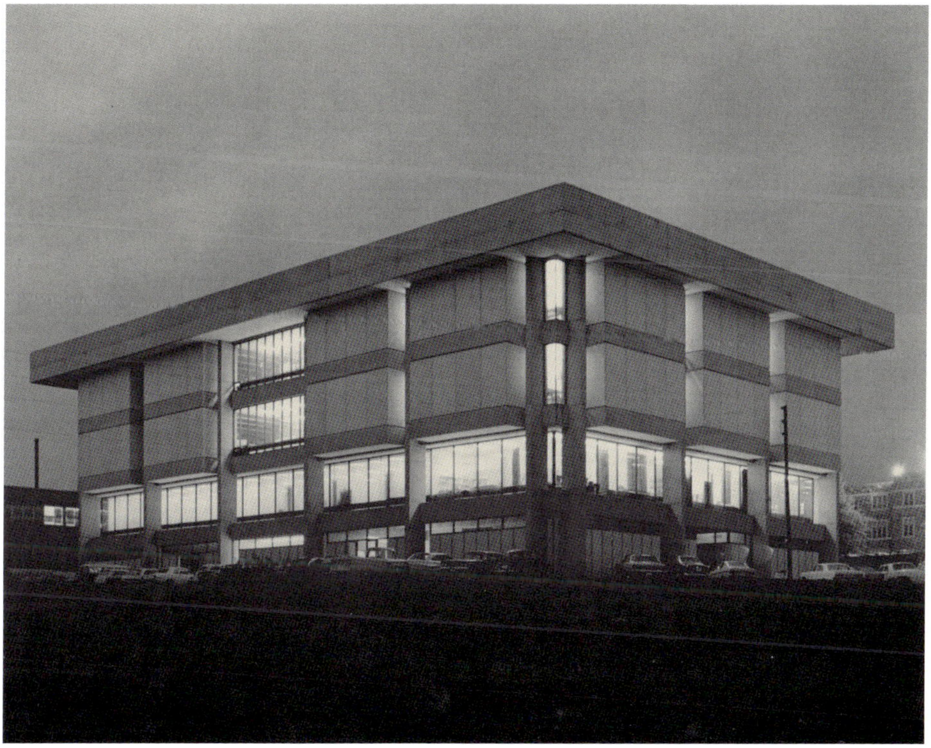

Cowgill Hall was completed in 1969 and was the first architecture building on campus as well as the first built in a style other than the traditional Collegiate Gothic used since the early 1900s. Cowgill Hall is named for Clinton Harriman Cowgill, the founder of the study of architecture at Virginia Tech, and is home to the College of Architecture and Urban Studies. The building was briefly occupied by student protesters after the Kent State uprising in 1970. (DLA.)

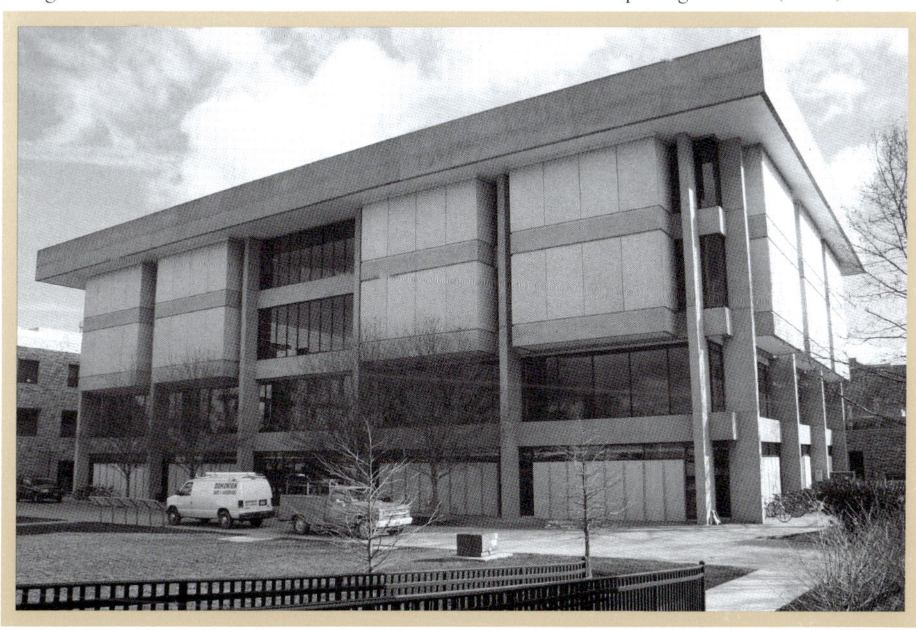

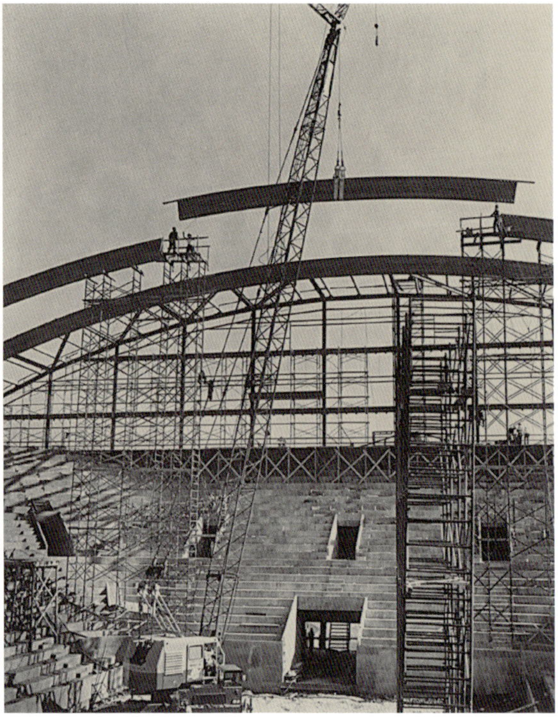

Cassell Coliseum was first used in early 1962, nearly three years prior to completion. The roof is supported by laminated wood arches that appear as concrete-covered flying buttresses on the exterior. Cassell Coliseum holds over 10,000 people and often reaches capacity for men's and women's ACC basketball games, commencement, concerts, and memorials. Lane Stadium can be seen in the background below. (DLA.)

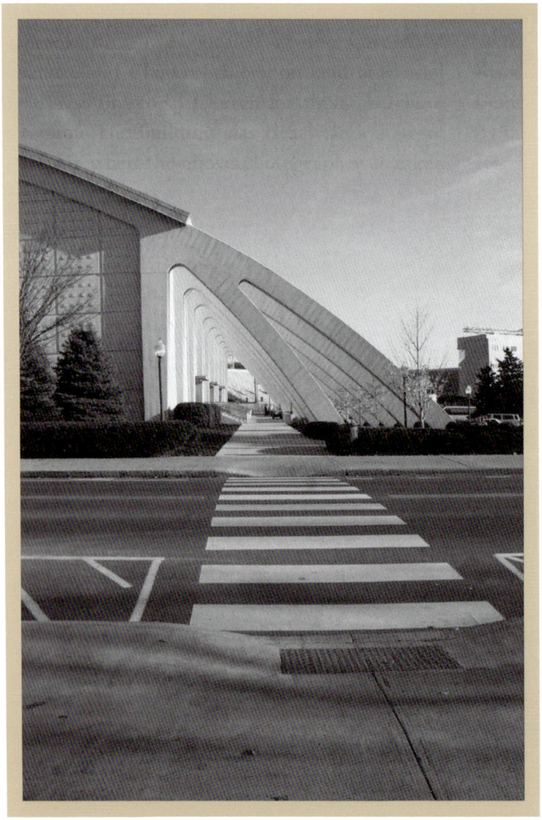

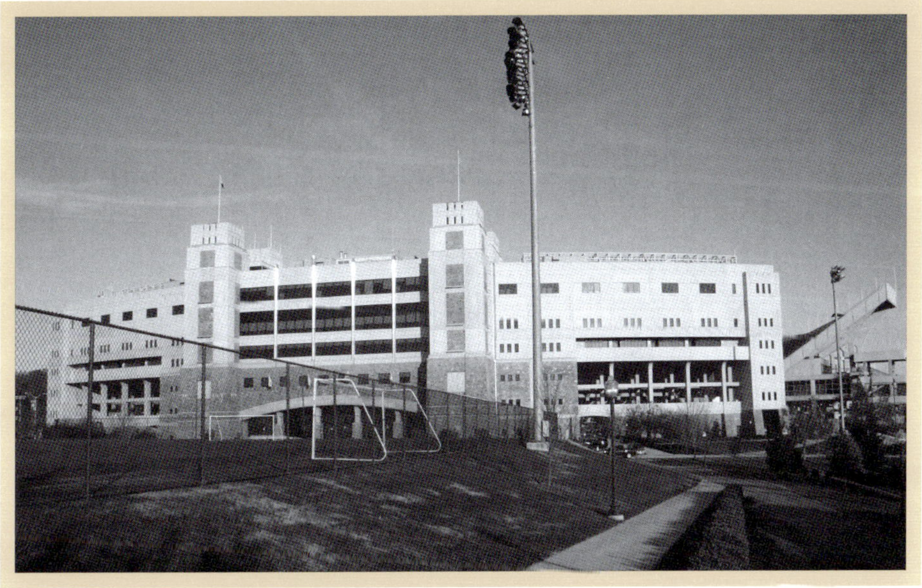

Lane Stadium and Worsham Field were first used in 1965 by the Virginia Tech football team. Seating 35,000 fans, the stadium replaced Miles Stadium, which had been in use since 1923. After a number of additions and expansions, Lane Stadium now seats 66,233 and is filled on fall Saturdays as fans cheer, "Lets Go Hokies!" (DLA.)

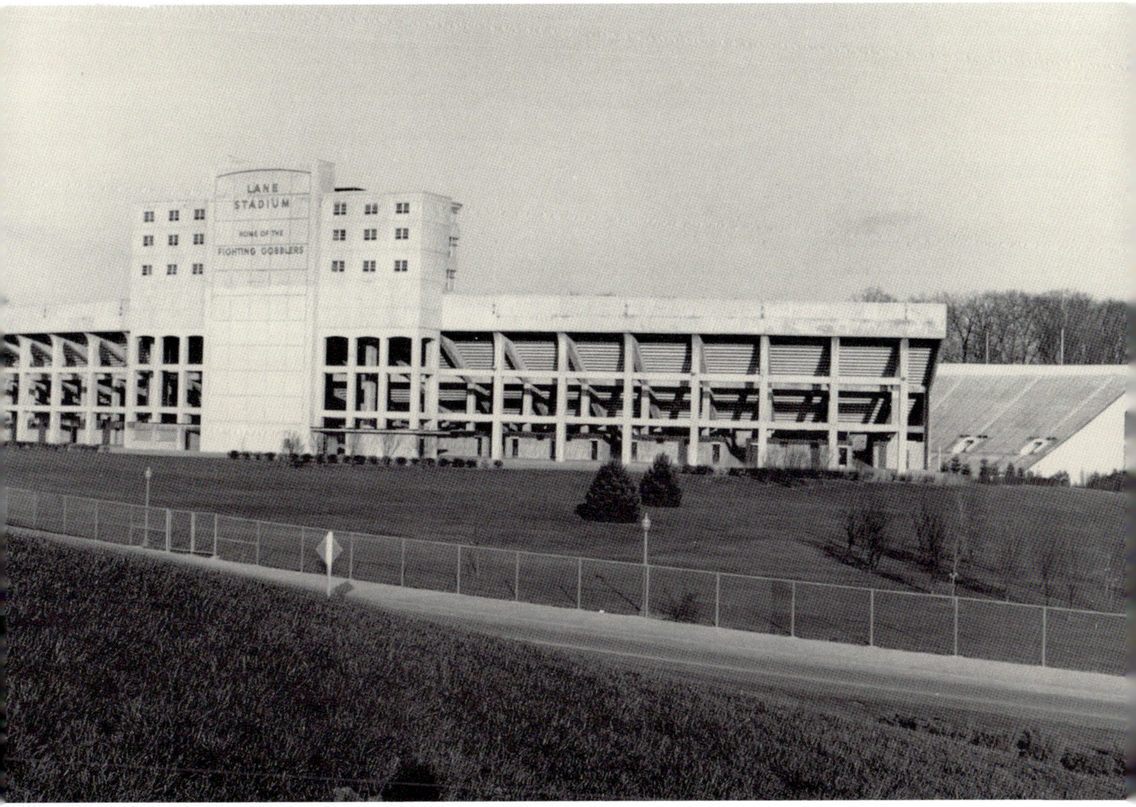